Finding and Following

Helen Oppenheimer

Finding and Following

Talking with children about God

SCM PRESS LTD

0 334 02579 6

First published 1994 by
SCM Press Ltd
26–30 Tottenham Road London N1 4BZ

Typeset at The Spartan Press Ltd
Lymington, Hampshire
Printed and bound in Great Britain by
Biddles Ltd, Guildford and King's Lynn

To

Nat	Patrick	Dorothy
Felix	Eleanor	Hannah
Scipio		Elsa
Noah		Lily

and remembering
Oliver

Contents

CONTENTS

Preface

This book is dedicated to my grandchildren and I hope that one day they will read it. In the meantime, I am trying to describe and explain the Christian faith which I hope they will learn to believe. This book is for adults who have some influence with children, which means almost all of us, and especially for people who are in touch with children: parents if they have any time to pause and think, grandparents, godparents, teachers, clergy and friends. I hope this book might also have something to say to people who have no particular connection with children at the moment but who can remember what it was like to be a child and ask childish questions.

I owe thanks to many people for encouragement and constructive criticism: my husband Michael throughout, and also several people who have read parts of my work at various stages, including my son-in-law, Ivo Mosley, my niece Patricia Brims, Mr Donald Whitton, Canon Eric Saxon and Father Clement Mullenger, SSM. The booklist is also a way of gratefully acknowledging indebtedness. I should also like to thank Dr John Bowden and Miss Margaret Lydamore of SCM Press for their encouraging helpfulness.

In quoting from the Bible I have generally used the Revised Standard Version, and for the Psalms I have used the Book of Common Prayer. The rather numerous notes are supposed to be a help, not a threat, to people who want to find references or to go further into these matters.

I

Children Finding God?

. . . it takes all the running you can do, to keep in the same place.

Lewis Carroll, *Through the Looking-Glass*

Could do better

This book is indirectly for children. It arises from a mixture of faith and concern. The faith is Christian faith. I am setting other faiths respectfully aside, because one cannot explore every question simultaneously. There are questions which need to be explored about how to understand the Christian faith and commend it to the next generation. It is part of Christian faith that people matter, because they are 'children of God'. To treat children as children of God is not as obvious as it sounds. It ought to rule out patronizing them, fobbing them off with soothing stories, stereotyping them, or using them for our own greater glory.

The concern is not despondency or alarm, but has an urgency none the less. It is a concern about the responsibility we all have for each other, to honour one another and indeed to cherish and encourage one another. For people who are fortunate enough to have faith, part of this responsibility is to pass on their faith in good order to the next generation. I do not think that at the moment we are doing this very well.

This is not, at least not directly, a judgment about what is going on or ought to go on in schools, still less a criticism of actual schools, many of which are happy, humane, well-organized places from which to begin to explore the world. Even less is it a judgment on parents, who on the whole get too much blame when things go wrong with their children and too much credit when things go well. Easy stereotypes of success and failure sap the self-confidence of people in the thick of the struggle and feed the complacency of people who are able to stand back and look on. Preconceived notions about 'Christian families' versus the world are apt to be distinctly unhelpful.

Christian faith ought to be a strength, not a hindrance. It should be a matter of concern to all of us who call ourselves Christians that so many people are being crippled by inadequate notions of the Christian faith, both in their own attempts to live as they should and in their hopes of imparting credible beliefs to their children.

Taking sides

'Impart' is notoriously problematic. We know that in-doctrinating children is wrong: we must not condition them into belief, especially religious belief. So ought religious teachers to be neutral, setting the options out plainly but objectively, and then leaving the children to choose for themselves, all in good time? To introduce Christianity like that without taking sides would certainly be a difficult challenge: more like explaining the difference between Cavaliers and Roundheads than teaching children to tell the time.

In fact religious neutrality is an impossible challenge. I can be neutral about Cavaliers and Roundheads, because whichever way my sympathies lie I cannot now join either side. It is straightforward to say 'on the one hand . . . on the other hand': 'Wrong but Wromantic . . . Right but Repulsive'.[1] Teacher and pupils can sit happily on this fence for ever. But religious belief is a live option. If I am not religious, the only practical alternative is to be non-religious. Even if I evade the likely question 'Do *you* believe this?' I cannot leave open the question, 'Does it matter?' If it matters, the question of truth cannot be by-passed for ever, or even for long. To leave children to decide for themselves is to come down on one side of this fence. Whatever message they are meant to receive, the message they *will* receive is, 'If this were the Truth, it would matter enough for me to give you more help.' If religious teaching does not move even one step towards saying,

'Oh taste, and see, how gracious the Lord is',[2] it has missed the point of the faith it purports to teach.

The demand for neutrality is a demand for agnosticism: it ought to rule out all the people who think they know the answer, believers and atheists alike, as teachers of religious knowledge. But the message which will come across is the atheist message. Belief will go by default, since the agnostic message in practice converges upon the atheist 'No'. Is indoctrination inevitable then, for or against? That would be defeatist. There is a true objectivity which does not claim an impossible neutrality, but plays fair and declares an interest.[3] It is hopeless to try to pretend to have no opinions. Even to children it ought to be possible to say, 'This is what I believe. Lots of people disagree. Ask them what they think.' If that is going to muddle them, it must muddle them still more to say, 'This is what children ought to believe but never mind: it doesn't have anything much to do with grown-up life.'

Stories for children

Children have plenty to muddle them. Because they are supposed to be too young for theology, they are offered a curious mixture of myth and morality. The myths as taught are plainly in conflict with the facts of science, and the facts of science are more interesting because they are more mind-stretching. Much of the morality is plainly in conflict with common sense and is easily characterized as 'goody-goody'. The world is made in six days; two famous people called Adam and Eve are disobedient; God suddenly decides to destroy everybody except one family and a menagerie of animals: that is the Old Testament. Baby Jesus comes; when he grows up he goes about doing good, which mostly means curing everyone's illnesses by magic; he tells us to turn the other cheek and to ask him for everything we want: that is the New Testament. None of this is connected with dinosaurs or spaceships or what to do when somebody is unkind to a friend of yours. Of course this caricature is not what anyone plans to teach children about Christianity, but when what they happen to learn is more chance than plan, assorted half-truths can gain a kind of arbitrary ascendancy.

3

Any Bible story with animals in it is irresistible to grown-ups who want to feel that they are doing something about the religious education of the little ones. So God creates all the animals and saves them in Noah's Ark, and the shiny picture-book which tells the story is classified as 'non-fiction'. Jonah is swallowed by a whale and sicked up again safe and sound. Mary rides to Bethlehem on a trusty donkey, and is encouraged by the ox and the ass when she has no comfortable place for her Baby to be born; and at last Jesus rides into Jerusalem on another donkey for the children to cry 'Hosanna'. Add a few sheep and a kind Shepherd, and we have described a selection of the most readily available theological equipment with which children are expected to face the troubled world in which they will have to live.

Protecting children

Civilized people like to think that they value and cherish children today more than they were valued and cherished in earlier times. The ideal of progress includes a kinder appreciation of children and childhood, compared with tougher and harsher attitudes in the past. The instinctive determination to love and protect one's offspring is not new, but now there has developed the perception that children ought to be happy here and now. Of course we want them not to be hurt; but also we want them not to be sad or frightened. We hope to protect them not only from damage but also from distress and alarm.

Old attitudes to childhood are not abandoned but combined with the new. The new conviction that children have the right to happiness is superimposed upon the old conviction that children must depend upon their elders. The upshot is the belief that the elders can and should filter the facts which children are to be told, and even the experiences which they are to be allowed to have, through a mesh of suitability.

Late twentieth-century civilization has been skilled at inventing ways of cushioning people from unpleasant facts. It is only too tempting to imagine that we can keep children, at least, in naive unawareness of anything nasty. Since so many aspects of the world are still by any standards 'unsuitable for children', and since children are naturally fascinated by what the grown-ups deem unsuitable, this hope itself is naive. Unrealistic cushioning makes a precarious basis for establishing a faith to live by.

The Christian faith is founded upon the cross and the resurrection. The cross, of all events in history, is unsuitable for children: but it happened. Those of us who believe that the resurrection is real too will never explain what we mean by it if the cross has to be left out. Adults who have formed the habit of using suitability as a criterion are tempted to evade the issue, skimp the foundations, and set up instead various more or less pleasing superstructures without adequate protection against storms.

It is easy to affirm as an elementary summary of what Christians believe, 'Jesus loves you', or 'Jesus is your Friend'. But on the whole children are not given to talking much about 'love'. To be loved is to be tucked up with a cuddle at bedtime and kissed better when you have hurt yourself. Loving means giving people beautiful surprises on their birthdays, and minding about the things they mind about. Talking about love is both unnecessary and embarrassing. Meanwhile a friend is somebody you play with and look forward to seeing, who argues with you and has the same ideas of fun. Children can see for themselves, although they may be too well-behaved to say, that Jesus does not love you like that and that a Friend is quite different from a friend. So they learn to make tacit distinctions between the different kinds of things that grown-up people tell them. Religion lives in a region of its own, where everything is a bit misty compared with the real world of nice and nasty people and places, where there are things to eat and switches to press, houses and shops and cars.

This lesson about religion and real life has been learnt by most of us and many of us never entirely unlearn it. In E. Nesbit's story *The Phoenix and the Carpet* the children mend the wear and tear in the magic carpet with heather-mixture fingering, which naturally has no special properties, so that people who travel on the thin places are only partly there. Their predicament could be an image for the patchy faith which half-supports a good many Christians, young and older. This kind of unreality bedevils communication between the laity and the clergy, who find it baffling that lay people do not appear to apply their religion to their daily lives.

Wrapping up reality

Almost two thousand years after Christ came, Father Christmas can seem more real than the heavenly Father, and a good deal more cheerful. Curiously enough, the reduced Christian faith which is easily imbibed by children is not characteristically a happy faith. Attempts to filter out anything frightening or painful seem to filter out anything really delightful as well. Shielding people from being alarmed may merely give them plenty of scope for being bored. When fears are kept under, hopes are smothered too. Human emotions, positive and negative, are like wheat and tares, too closely entangled for simple weeding. So we have an odd reversal: Christianity comes across as soothing where it should be strenuous and gloomy where it should be joyful.

Among grown-up people death may be less of a taboo than it was, but even devout Christians would prefer to protect children from thoughts about human mortality. If death is too fearful to mention and yet has to be faced, of course it is tempting to translate it as 'going to heaven'. So heaven, like most euphemisms, loses its own meaning and is down-graded into a synonym for something unpleasant.

Christian reluctance to think about heaven may have a more creditable explanation. Besides unwillingness to face fear, there is a wholesome reaction against oversimplified hope. Too much 'heavenly comfort' has been naive, cloying, macabre or even manipulative. To outgrow shallow otherworldliness may be uncomfortable but is not faithless.

When confidence is in short supply, for better or worse reasons, a sort of vague reverence takes over, which half-affirms the angels on their clouds, the harps and the waiting around all in white, but fails to recognize any future for beloved pets and childish fun.[4] Instead of looking hopefully at real life to find live images of heaven, grown-ups feel obliged to discount children's everyday doings as babyish. Meanwhile they remain reticent about their own real hopes and fears, partly because they have not thought them out. Their negations come through strongly, as more sophisticated than their expurgated faith. It is no wonder that what the children pick up is the scepticism which is meant to be hidden from them.

If the Christian faith were only an assortment of euphoric legends, it really would be unsuitable for children and adults alike. It must be wrong to feed children upon insincerities about our deepest beliefs, where the very heart of grown-up truthfulness ought to be. It must be stupid to think that the little ones are too stupid to notice. Part of growing up is realizing that grown-ups are not all-wise. To join an adult world full of fallible human beings is an enfranchisement; but to discover that the people who say they know best are cheating is a disillusionment. There is a world of difference between 'They don't know' and 'They don't care.' What Christians of all ages need rather than naivety is a kind of faithful agnosticism which says 'There's a great deal we do not know: but all things are possible with God.'[5]

2

Behaving

The antidote to sin is not duty but praise.

David Jenkins[1]

Caricatures

There is a half-truth that religion is 'better caught than taught'. Of course example is far better than precept: but first a foundation has to be laid. To believe is to believe something, and we do need to know what. 'Caught not taught' is misleading if it suggests that faith has nothing much to do with facts and that becoming a believer is like coming out in spots.

What is the meaning of Christian faith? At least three questions are packed up in this: What do Christians affirm? Are these affirmations true? and, Does it matter? A little girl who had been an angel in a nativity play was asked whether she knew what Jesus did when he grew up. She thought for a moment and answered, 'He walked on the water.' Whatever her elders believe about miracles, they would surely all agree that walking on the water was not the main thing Jesus did: but what was? This is where people start to say to children, 'He went about doing good': that is, he told people to be kind to each other and he cured their troubles by doing miracles. But when the grown-ups do not see fit to add, 'And they killed him,' they have left themselves nothing much to say about his rising from the dead, except that he is up in heaven now, keeping an eye on us. So Jesus looks after us by answering our prayers and is always watching to see that we keep the rules.

This caricature of Christian faith is a junior version of a familiar, and misleading, set of assumptions about how faith, providence and moral values fit together. God looks after us, so

everything that happens to us must be according to plan; likewise
our ancient values are safe so long as God provides backing for
morality at the highest level; and the reason why Christianity
matters is that without it people, that is other people, will not
know the difference between right and wrong. We know our
religion is true, because it gives meaning to our lives. We have to
believe in Christianity because 'only such a faith can outlast the
death of old cultures . . . ' C. S. Lewis' devil took the point: 'You
see the little rift? "Believe this, not because it is true, but for some
other reason."'[2]

Faith and values

What sort of faith is it which has in fact lasted through twenty
centuries? Jesus loves us, God looks after us: but how? The
caricatures, junior and senior, have taken such a hold lately, like
bindweed, that they are obscuring the view and need to be dug
out properly: which will be hard work and may appear quite
negative at first. Why not let the weeds grow, especially when
they have such pretty flowers? Enjoying a quick crop of goodness
and kindness mixed up with trust in providence seems more
rewarding than a back-breaking struggle to cultivate theology.

More seriously, many people think of theology itself as a
thorny growth strangling true religion. They ask what the niceties
of dogma matter compared with moral values. Looking around,
they see on the one hand pedantic traditionalists, concentrating
on correct belief, and on the other hand woolly liberals,
concentrating on giving people what they want. Either way,
'Christian standards' seem to go by default. Surely the heart of
true religion is doing what one ought? When children grow up
not understanding the difference between right and wrong, it
seems obvious that the churches must be to blame. The cry goes
up, 'Back to the Ten Commandments.'

Of course morality is central in our faith. The Bible constantly
links knowledge of God with obedience to God's will. Christianity was at first called 'the way'. Much further back, right back to
the origins of our tradition in tribal religion, the children of Israel
worshipped a God who was always conspicuously concerned

with good and evil. Nothing is more fundamental in the religion we profess than the belief that God's holiness is also righteousness, requiring righteousness of human beings in the form of justice and mercy and regard for one another. We can read the Bible as the record of how God's people were educated to understand God's goodness.

But God's goodness is much more than 'thou shalt not', or even 'thou shalt'. The Ten Commandments are set in the context of the Covenant God made with the children of Israel.[3] God has rescued the people from Egypt and promises them faithful love. The people are called to respond with faithful gratitude. In all the subsequent history their loyalty is patchy but never quite lost. 'Back to the Ten Commandments' loses half its point if it gives sole priority to obedience without giving children glimpses of 'the breadth and length and height and depth'[4] of God's love.

There are various reasons why people who care about standards are feeling beleaguered today. Besides the ordinary worry of ageing moralists about the non-conformist behaviour of the young, there are real and strong pressures upon moral values, coming from the dangerous mixture of a lot of well-meaning naivety, and some self-seeking wickedness. The naivety assumes that human beings are good really, even without being taught how. The wickedness trades on their actual badness.

People are not very good, but often they would like to be good, whether they believe in God or not. Values ought not to be a monopoly of the churches. Basic morality should be something we have in common as human beings. It is entirely logical, though naive in practice, to expect unbelievers, just as much as believers, to acknowledge the sovereignty of good. Unfortunately the conviction that right and wrong are real is under just as much pressure as belief in God.

It is not inept Christians but moral philosophers who have effectively instructed twentieth-century people that morality is a matter of choice. Philosophy has found, or made, a great divide between the facts we find and the values we choose, and it is still quite hard to cross this chasm.[5] The spirit of the age has orthodoxies as strict as religious dogmas. Facts are objective, but values are one's own choice.[6] People who choose God choose

God's values: the others must make up their own. On this view the strongest moral duty is to be an autonomous moral being, and religious people are under suspicion that they are not properly autonomous.

So just at a time when Christian allegiance looks like a hobby for a minority, large numbers of human beings with no such allegiance are supposed to decide for themselves what they will take for good and evil. The confidently high-minded, and the unscrupulous, may be pleased with do-it-yourself morality. 'Now I can be truly autonomous.' 'Now I can do what I want.' Meanwhile plenty of people of good will are alarmed when they see what is going on.

Anyone who cares about values should be bold enough to affirm that values are real in their own right. Instead, believers and unbelievers alike seem to go along with the defeatist assumption that if religion fails objective right and wrong are bound to collapse too. So religion must not be allowed to fail. People who sit fairly loose to creeds still want the Gospel to be preached, as a prop for our values. Then they blame the churches for the chaotic morality of our times.

Moralism

Frightened people miss opportunities. The maxim 'better caught than taught' really could come into its own when standards are at risk. Children and grown-ups need to be shown what goodness is, rather than instructed in morality. But people who are seized with the importance of defending good order against wild liberal follies fall back nervously upon saying 'Teach children the difference between right and wrong', instead of demonstrating how attractive goodness can be.

Teaching right and wrong generally means telling people what to do: and most people are fairly resistant to being told what to do. Moral instruction cannot get far without using the word 'ought', which is extremely likely in practice to come through as nagging. Dutiful goodness is not very catching.

If the nagging is ascribed to God's will, Christianity itself shrinks. When most of the theology has already been filtered out, not much of Christianity is left except dutiful goodness. The cross has been put aside because it is unpleasant, and moral uplift is offered as a happier substitute: providing a gloom of its own for the little ones who are supposed to be protected. Moralists may be surprised. Surely the days of hell-fire preaching are gone, and sweetness and light prevail, almost to a fault. But the deadliness of moralism has little to do either with threats of hell, or with the denial of hell.

Moralism is a sort of flattening of morality, in which questions about the best way to live are answered by permissions or prohibitions. 'You may spend your pocket money on what you like.' 'You mustn't say what is not true.' Children's minds are easily moulded by the grown-up attitude that obedience and naughtiness are the primary ethical categories. The God of this kind of religion is mainly concerned with making rules and watching to see whether people keep them.

Moralism is not the same thing as rigorism, although they may overlap. Rigorism is an attempt to put into practice, at whatever cost, the belief that nothing short of perfection is good enough for God. For rigorists, compromise looks like a worldly snare, and hard cases make bad law. So rigorists are apt to be beset by a negative fear of disobedience. That is how a heroic quest for goodness can begin to be corrupted into moralism.

When people take the will of God really seriously, it is hardly surprising that they blame people who care less. So righteousness slips easily into self-righteousness. Rigorism applied to oneself wobbles on the edge of priggishness. 'I could not consider behaving like that.' Rigorism applied to other people invites rebellion. 'Why should *you* tell *me* what to do?' Rebellion invites condemnation: and condemning other people feeds the conviction that one knows best. So rigorism may come to be manifested as moralistic self-esteem.

But people who cannot bear rigorism and react into permissiveness are still caught in the same trap. There is not much to choose between the rigorist 'You may not' and the permissive 'You may'. 'What can I get away with?' is part of the same way of seeing the world as 'What must I do?' Whether the answer is to be strict or lenient, the generous enquiry 'What can I do?' is swamped. The warmth and enthusiasm of real goodness, or even badness, are cooled into 'nicely calculated less or more'.[7] With the most lofty intentions, generous giving, and generous taking too, are lost in bargaining. Rights and duties, which are the necessary framework to support human life as it ought to be, come to look like the whole substance of human life as it ought to be.

A simple test may reveal how Christian morality can be moralistically diminished. Everyone loves, and identifies as truly 'Christian', the parables of the Good Samaritan and the Prodigal Son.[8] To go about doing good, or to sin and repent and be forgiven by our loving Father: these are the most easily recognizable ways of being a Christian. The parable of the Sower[9] who cast the seed on different kinds of soil is not so comfortable, but one feels at home with it as an analysis of human failure. But the parable of the Labourers in the Vineyard,[10] in which the latecomers are paid as much as the ones who have worked all day, worries people: not that human goodness fails to measure up to the demands of Christ, but that Christ seems to fail to measure up to human goodness. 'It's not fair.' And when one comes to think about it, the Prodigal Son is worrying too. He goes home when he gets hungry. Is he really sorry, or is his repentance just cupboard love? His father does not wait to make sure.

The answer to both worries is 'That is exactly the point.' Moralism works out what people deserve and makes claims on their behalf. 'Surely it's time I had some reward.' 'Behaviour like that must be well punished.' If all else fails, repentance can be a claim. 'You ought to forgive me now that I've said I'm sorry.' But the teaching of Christ is that all human claims are swallowed up in the generosity of God. When people start to ask what right he had to make this huge affirmation, that is the moment for the reply, 'He backed it up with his life, and was vindicated by his rising from death.'

3

Believing

We shall trust him, if he exists, but we can hardly trust him to exist. We must have reason to think that he does.

Austin Farrer[1]

Searching

If grown-up Christians could spell out their belief more distinctly they could say, 'This is what young Christians need to know: please, teachers, will you find out how to teach it?' It may be impossible to teach theology directly to children, but what the grown-ups believe, half-believe or disbelieve will get through to the children, not always in ways anyone intends or wants.

There is a curious blend of vagueness and assertiveness which takes the name of the Lord in vain. Believers play safe by deploring 'dogma', but admit no uncertainty. Vagueness looks reverent and firmness sounds faithful; but the mixture is not a good cure for doubt. God would be more honoured if people who count themselves as Christians put the confidence and the reverence the other way round. A faith which was bold enough to make some more specific statements could afford to make them more tentatively.

Vagueness is not more reverent than definiteness. When people begin to find, like St Thomas Aquinas, that in the face of God's reality everything they have tried to say so far is like straw, they may become inarticulate but they will not become vague. The remedy for presumption is more likely to be careful honesty about what little we can say, with acknowledgment of how little it is, than smooth platitudes which cannot be untrue because they are not saying anything in particular.

It is fashionable for thinking Christians to be quite ashamed of the creeds because they dare to make definite statements, but perhaps the shame is misplaced. The creeds state what the Christian church believes. They are 'dogma' in the old sense of doctrine propounded, and would be none the worse for that, were it not for the human tendency to add arrogance to affirmation and make dogma dogmatic.

The creeds invite people to say 'Yes'. Some say 'No', or 'I don't know', or even, 'I don't understand.' Others may say 'Yes – in part' and discuss rewriting. It cannot be irrelevant or irreverent to ask 'How do you know?' People who are able to say 'Yes' with certainty ought to remember that a creed is not the whole truth. From God's point of view creeds are baby-talk.

If human beings can say anything about God at all, if there is a God about whom anything can be said, the first principle must be that God is much greater than we can imagine. Confident platitudes fail in two ways to suggest God's greatness. Platitudes say nothing about God worth saying, while confidence seems to presume that we have God buttoned up.

There is nothing wrong with saying, to grown-ups or children, 'Let's try to find out.' People who have reached the point of saying 'I believe' may still say it tentatively. To accept a creed provisionally, as a working hypothesis, hoping for further illumination, is neither self-contradictory nor irreverent. It was St Anselm, not a twentieth-century liberal, who said, 'I believe in order that I may understand.'

Belief is a word with a range of meanings along a spectrum: from the almost agnostic plea for help of the father of the epileptic boy, 'I believe; help my unbelief';[2] by way of the caution of St Thomas who made a condition, 'Unless I see the mark of the nails . . . I will not believe';[3] to the assurance attained by the Beloved Disciple who saw and believed.[4] 'I believe' means 'Here I put my faith,' or even, 'Here I take sides.'

'I believe' and 'I know' are not synonyms, though belief may grow firmer and converge upon knowledge. As an aspiring affirmation of first-hand experience, people say things like, 'I know that my Redeemer liveth': but that works as a slogan rather than a creed. Nobody knows what it meant in its original context.[5] Christians have adopted it. Wonderfully set to music, it has become a radiant announcement of trust in Christ, an encouragement to believers. If this 'I know' is treated as if it were instruction for unbelievers, it becomes 'dogmatic' in the disreputable sense.

Reason and faith

Christians cannot escape the demand to give a reason for the hope that is in them.[6] Sometimes they have felt obliged to try to 'prove the existence of God', taking it for granted that giving reasons must mean providing proofs. It is not surprising that this enterprise has never been particularly successful. As we are not to test God or manage God, it is entirely in keeping that we are unable to prove God. It would be surprising if human beings were able to produce plain arguments capable of convincing all comers who are not stupid or recalcitrant. If God's existence could be so definitely established, ordinary life would have to be lived on quite a different basis. If human beings were always distinctly aware of Somebody watching, how could they act sincerely or grow morally?

The most famous 'proofs', such as St Thomas Aquinas' 'Five Ways', do not work as mathematical demonstrations. They can be used as explanations of what is meant by talk about God, as accounts of what God is believed to be like. The best response is not 'Q.E.D.' but 'I see the idea.' What we ought to hope for, and encourage young Christians to hope for, is not a proof but enough to go on. A cumulative case built up slowly is more promising than a clinching argument.[7]

Although demonstrating can mean proving mathematically, in everyday speech it means *showing*. 'O taste, and see, how gracious the Lord is'[8] is an invitation, not a theorem. Aiming at proof can be a distraction from setting out what there is, so to say, on offer. Not expecting to prove allows honourable scope for trying to convince. There are plenty of considerations, drawn from the past and the present, which Christians can offer in commendation of their faith and in answer to objections. They ought not to be manipulative and it does them no credit to be dogmatic.

Certainty in the form of overwhelming religious experience seems to be given to some people, generally not for their own especial benefit but for the encouragement of others. In all this, said Julian of Norwich,

> I was greatly moved in love towards my fellow Christians, that they might all see and know the same as I saw, for I wished it to be a comfort to them, for all this vision was shown for all men.[9]

Assurance does not mean the same as peace. Prophets characteristically have stormy lives. Particularly clear weather is said to be a sign of rain on the way; but most of us can expect to live, and can be content to live, in more hazy conditions in which we catch glimpses of truth.

The Christian faith carries conviction as a coherent whole which is capable of sustaining grown-up people. The best way to convince the next generation of its truth is to offer it as a whole, as the best way to explain how things are, and give it a chance to convince.

Doubt and faith

Many people find this approach much too complicated and uncertain. Surely the faith which has lasted down the centuries must be a simple faith, which ordinary people and children can understand, rooted in the teaching of Christ about trusting our heavenly Father? Why do people who call themselves Christian struggle and fret, and puzzle their minds about finding a creed to live by, instead of walking humbly with their God? Why do followers of Jesus seem unable to adopt the directness of the faith of Jesus?

For innocently plain believers this difficulty does not arise, and heaven forbid that sophisticated fellow-disciples should cause them to stumble. But in the late twentieth century many of us, grown-ups and children, are sophisticated. The problem makes itself felt whether we like it or not.

In these conditions the plea, 'Help my unbelief', presents itself hopefully as a favourite text. It looks just what we need, but cannot be the whole answer. Anyone who tries to settle down here will soon come under pressure from opposite directions. On one side, straightforward fellow-Christians disapprove of acknowledging any unbelief. They know at first hand what trustful faith means: why make it all so difficult? On the other side, straightforward sceptics understand only too well the reasons for untrustful doubt: whatever Jesus said, we all know that rosy confidence will never answer in the real world. Between 'You ought to believe' and 'You ought not to believe, and after all you don't', it is no wonder that less simple Christians are uncertain and sometimes evasive.

'Whatever Jesus said'. We do not know exactly what Jesus said, but there is no escape that way from the difficulty. We do know that he uttered some hard sayings, and for twentieth-century Christians among the hardest is the plain message of simple faith. 'Go into your room and shut the door and pray to your Father who is in secret.'[10] 'Fear not, little flock, for it is your Father's good pleasure to give you the kingdom.'[11] If these are not the very words of the Lord, there are plenty more sayings on the same lines.

It looks as if Jesus encouraged a directness which we cannot achieve. Do we have the unhappy choice between being defeatist with the sceptics, naive with the fundamentalists, vague with the uninstructed, or too clever with the radicals? It is fair to approach this question by asking another. *To what question is simple faith the answer?* Jesus was not addressing sceptics. He was not talking about how to find God but about how to live with God. His hearers already believed firmly in God but needed to learn about what God is like. He was talking to virtuous people who thought God belonged to them, and sinful people who were afraid of God. 'Trust your heavenly Father' is not a way of curing doubt: it is a prescription for the legalism of the righteous and the timidity of sinners. The people around Jesus had a long tradition of confidence that God exists, and the message to them was, 'Live up to your faith! Trust the God you believe in! Be ready to understand that God does new things!'

People today are beset by questions about belief in contrast to unbelief. They apply to themselves the teaching of Jesus about trustfulness, and find it hard, not helpful. It seems safest to smother their doubts, and at least not hand their worries on to the next generation. What they do hand on is a feeling that doubts are both frightening and morally reprehensible. Over-protectiveness creates the dangers it fears. 'There is no cause for alarm' is particularly conducive to alarm.

There is no need to sow doubt in anybody's mind, but it is sensible to realize how naturally questions grow. John Lucas suggested in a sermon that

> doubt is the form in which many Christians in the present age are called upon to share in the sufferings of mankind after the example of our Lord.

He has hope to offer:

> Faith comes from God, and may not have come to you yet; but though you cannot be a believer just by choosing, you can be a doer just by choosing; though you cannot be a Christian, you can by a settled determination of the will be a would-be Christian.[12]

Maybe Browning's Bishop Blougram ought to have been a seeker rather than a bishop, but his question is not cynical:

> 'What think you of Christ', friend? when all's done and said
> Like you this Christianity or not?
> It may be false, but will you wish it true?
> Has it your vote to be so if it can?[13]

Tentativeness need not be timid; and caution need not be lukewarm. Exploration is not a revolt against the truth but a search for truth. If we really want to find we shall probably have to seek.

There is no need to resort to blind leaps in the dark as the only alternative to rational proof. People who contrast 'faith' with 'reason' are apt to suppose that they must give up the one or the other. Religion has to be 'a matter of faith' for those who can swallow it, while rational human beings have to be sceptics. This misunderstanding drives many people away from faith and leaves others inhabiting castles in the air, with no visible means of support.

Rational human beings feel safe when they can start with clear known premises and build up firm conclusions. Surely unless every stone we lay rests securely on solid foundations the cathedral will never stand up? This is not quite true even within the terms of the architectural analogy. An arch is propped up with temporary wooden centring until the keystone is lowered into place and bonds the whole together. Many people's Christian faith is held up in this provisional way by centring, or we might say by shuttering, which encloses concrete until it sets firm. This condition may be quite uncomfortable but is not dishonest or irresponsible.

To praise simple faith can even be misleading when people suppose that all anyone needs is elementary faith, suitable for beginners. In the late twentieth century it takes a good deal of maturity to win through to an honest and firmly-based trustfulness, distinct from naivety. To be properly trustful, people need to have found out what, or rather who, is trustworthy.

This emphasis should be optimistic. It would be gloomy only if the necessary maturity were a discouragingly rare gift. Maturing is growing up. Attaining to maturity is ordinary and straightforward, but needs time: there is no quick short cut to it. Asking questions, far from being a faithless aberration of sophisticated rebels, is the way children learn, including, we are told, the Lord himself.[14] It is uphill work to teach anything to people who are not asking questions.

'Secularization' is supposed to mean that people who would have had a simple faith in the old days are questioning everything now in the light of scientific knowledge. On the whole the contrary is true: it is the inquisitive learners who have seemingly disappeared. People fail to enquire into Christianity when they deem it to be not so much false as boring. A little test will make this apparent. Imagine telling a group of children that 'gospel' means 'good news'. Would their faces light up, or would a glazed look come into their eyes? Somehow a generation has been inoculated against live faith with small doses of harmless vaccine.

In Hans Andersen's story of the Emperor's New Clothes, the Emperor had nothing on at all, and it took a small child to point this out. Believers whose faith is no confidence trick ought to be glad of people who become as little children and ask awkward questions. If everyone shuts up, whether nervously or reverently, the truth goes by default. Even if the Emperor is splendidly arrayed, he might just as well have nothing on, if what he is told will be the same either way.

Trusting

If we get rid of credulity, shall we destroy the happy play of imagination? Shall we ban the psalm which announces, 'The Lord is King, and hath put on glorious apparel: the Lord hath put on his apparel, and girded himself with strength.'[15] We do not want some prosaic person to come along and point out that of course God does not wear clothes.

What the small child punctures is unreality, not poetry. The Emperor's new clothes were imaginary, not imaginative: figments, not figures of speech. He put them on in the expectation that they would literally keep out the rain. The Christian by contrast puts on the whole armour of God,[16] and is not at all surprised that it does not clank as he walks.

The shield of faith is a metaphorical way of finding words for an experience of protection against evil. When there is something definite to be said, figurative language may be the clearest way to say it. Poetry or prose can express truths or lies. Memorable, inspired, even holy teaching is as likely to be metaphorical as literal. Sceptics may think that there is no Good Shepherd, but they are not going to discourage believers by pointing out that human beings are not woolly sheep.

Some people have such literal minds that poetry is a real barrier for them in understanding truth. Some people take refuge in literal-mindedness when they would rather not understand. Nicodemus' question, whether someone 'can enter a second time into his mother's womb and be born', seems somewhere between the two and earns a gentle rebuke.[17]

What is blameworthy is to block out belief, not to find belief hard. Scepticism is not sinful, unless scepticism takes the form of bigotry: which however it is quite apt to do. To be sceptical and to be bigoted are not contraries. Bigots do not always believe too much while sceptics believe too little. On the contrary, religious bigotry can be a kind of mirror image of unbelieving bigotry, a more subtle way of showing lack of faith. Bigoted sceptics refuse to open their eyes to see what might be there, while bigoted believers wear blinkers to shut out fresh understanding of the faith they claim to possess.

If honest doubt is no sin, why is belief so warmly commended in the Gospels, to the alarm of people of integrity today? Many preachers try to answer this question by contrasting 'believing' and 'believing in', and singling out only 'believing in' for praise. The distinction is valid but has come to sound churchy. It can be put more bluntly. The simple faith Christians ought to have is quite different from credulity. It is faith as contrasted with fuss. There is a kind of faithlessness which has little to do with weighing up belief and unbelief. Doubt may say, 'That's unlikely' but faithlessness says, 'Oh dear, oh dear!'

Anyone who pays attention to the Sermon on the Mount as a summary of Christian morality can discover that worry is as unChristian as lust.[18] The disciples in the boat panicked when Jesus slept calmly on the cushion. 'Teacher, do you not care if we perish?'[19] By contrast, strangers recognized the authority of the Lord and surprised him by trusting in his power.[20] Having faith is not naively believing everything one is told, but putting one's heart into living by what one has seen so far.

One way to 'become as little children'[21] is to consider what lack of faith looks like from the heavenly Father's point of view. It is impossible to take a splinter out of a child's finger if she is squeaking with fright and pulling her hand away in a panic. The operation may hurt, but with trust it will hurt less and be over sooner.

Faith has a great deal to do with loyalty. In the last resort faith may require the loyalty of the martyr: but that is not where believers begin, any more than children learning their first sums begin with trigonometry. A more elementary lesson, a tiny 'religious experience', is to discover for oneself that the rebuke 'Why are you afraid? Have you no faith?'[22] is being almost teasingly applied to one's state of mind: not a reproach for doubt, but for fretfulness. First-century Galilee is a long way away, but sometimes one can dare to say, 'Thus saith the Lord: calm down, stop worrying.' Serenity may be more 'Christian' than passionate conviction.

It ought to be a platitude to say that the time for serenity is now. This platitude is quite hard to take to heart. People pray for grace to cope with tomorrow's trouble, and can hardly help muddling together 'Don't let it happen,' 'Help me to manage whatever does happen' and 'Thy will be done.' Even Omnipotence cannot answer such a confused prayer.[23] There cannot be grace for the emergency which has not happened yet. The prayer which makes sense is 'Help me now!' There can be help for present responsibility, present emotions, even present anxiety. People sometimes say, 'I couldn't bear *that*.' They ought not to try. If 'that' is something which has not yet arrived, it is the fear of 'that', not 'that' itself, which can be borne now by God's grace. Just as alcoholics are encouraged not to say 'I'll never have another drink' but 'I'll not have this drink,' so Christians need not try to store up grace for future contingencies.

Thanking

Fretfulness ought to be even more foreign to Christians than scepticism. This affirmation suddenly starts to go in the wrong direction, like the path in Looking Glass Land which 'gave a sudden twist, and shook itself'[24] and took Alice straight back into the house. Assumptions about what *ought* to be are apt to shake themselves and lead straight back into the moralistic caricature versions of Christianity. To say, 'Christians ought to be grateful, not fretful' loses sight of encouragement. 'You must cheer up and thank God for all your blessings even if you feel thoroughly downhearted.' The more bracing the exhortation, the more uncertainly one grasps the blessings.

Gratitude is not something people can force themselves to feel, still less something they can induce other people to feel, but a response to something which someone has done. Why do Christians thank God? Surely 'for being good' is not the answer, if God's goodness only makes us feel bad. Do Christians believe that God has done anything definite? Is Christian gratitude a kind of official thankfulness for everything? Is it even a servile refusal to object to anything that God might see fit to do?

In the Book of Common Prayer of the Church of England there is a summary statement of the reality of Christian gratitude: the General Thanksgiving. Here Christian people are invited to say thank you for 'all the blessings of this life'; but primarily they are encouraged to give thanks for what they believe God has done. Christians are grateful above all for God's 'inestimable love in the redemption of the world by our Lord Jesus Christ; for the means of grace, and for the hope of glory'.

For some of us this is almost a creed. Its dignified rhythmical language is resonant with faith, though it is simple enough to have been left unchanged in the Alternative Service Book. It picks out our basic belief. Our gratitude is not just lip-service to divine supremacy. We believe that God's love is not only 'inestimable' but literally down to earth.

For others, this is just the way old-fashioned churchy people talk. 'Redemption' is technical, 'our Lord' mediaeval, 'means of grace' irrelevant, and 'the hope of glory' unreal. Old-fashioned churchy people find it natural to use this language and can hardly see how it could be irrelevant or boring; but if they want to communicate with their younger contemporaries they cannot take these dignified phrases for granted. To be usable for communication, not just as a sort of incantation, language must say something which people can begin to understand.

Some words, such as 'redemption', will need to be translated. That is not the main problem. The antiquity, and indeed the technicality, of religious language would be manageable, if people had a lively wish to understand it. Old-fashioned believers complain that young people today are either too stupid or too uneducated to comprehend what our forbears took in their stride. What young people more urgently lack is the idea that all this is worth bothering with. 'There's no demand' for the concept that God makes us and saves us.

Is the terminology of the General Thanksgiving jargon? That might be its particular usefulness. It might be the kind of jargon, like computer jargon, which can inaugurate people into a way of life. They have to want to belong, but once they have the beginnings of enthusiasm the language is there to provide them with a framework, the skeleton of a living faith.

4

Cornerstone

. . . built upon the foundation of the apostles and prophets,
Christ Jesus himself being the chief corner stone.

Eph. 2.20

Belief in Christ

Christian faith takes many forms, but always has something to do
with a particular man, Jesus of Nazareth. Christians characteristically believe that God 'came down to earth from heaven' and
lived a human life. That belief is what traditional Christianity
offers to enquirers who are trying to see what sense can be made
of the world. If the first principle of the Christian faith[1] is that
God is much greater than we can imagine, there is a second
principle, that God comes to meet us. Any such talk about a God
who comes into the world needs justifying, of course, in terms of
the impact of Jesus upon his contemporaries: the conviction they
have communicated to the succeeding generations that 'God was
in Christ',[2] that here is someone so much 'greater than Solomon'[3]
that worship, not just admiration, is suitable.

There is a caricature of the Christian faith which alert
Christians will firmly repudiate, but which is still quite lively. It
contrasts God the stern Lawgiver of the Old Testament, who
wants to punish us, with Jesus the loving Saviour, who wants to
let us off. There are plenty of reasons why this caricature will not
do. The Trinity is not like this: Father, Son and Holy Spirit are
one God. Divine mercy is not like this: forgiveness is reconciliation, not compromise. The Old Testament is not like this: the
Law is 'sweeter than honey' to God's people.[4] Jesus is not like
this: 'gentle Jesus, meek and mild' is a travesty of the strong
character portrayed in the Gospels.

Although we may think that we have banished the caricature, it lingers around, or at least the notion of the kindly but depressingly good Jesus lingers around: and this figure is even more moralistic than the warrior God he displaces. He comes 'preaching the gospel of God' and the dreary connotations of 'preaching' obliterate the information that 'gospel' means 'good news'. Our sins make him sad, not angry. If we dutifully follow his example we shall often be sad and never angry. Though the terror and heroism of the passion are left out of this picture, the passiveness remains. He is the 'man of sorrows', who would never stand up for himself, who would never do anything just for fun, who would never see a joke. Even well-behaved people would rather this Lord were not watching their ordinary doings: indeed he is just what they mean by a spoilsport.

If this description rings true, it need not be an indictment of current Christian teaching. Of course it is a long time since anything like this was taught to children, if indeed it ever was. But too many people who count themselves as Christians have in the back of their minds, or even in the front of their minds, a dismal picture of Jesus Christ which they have somehow acquired in their childhood, and it is this picture which they will half-consciously impart to the next generation of children. Reverence perpetuates this imaginary figure by making it impossible to criticize him, let alone to realize that he is a fiction. Yet it should be easy to banish him. There is no need to go in for wish-fulfilment, or even for subtle argumentation. It is necessary only to read the New Testament with a fresh mind.

That sounds a dangerous thing to say when we all know how prone people are to read into the Bible what they want to find, and make Christ in their own image. Such confidence sounds alarmingly fundamentalist: do we really suppose that the Gospels give us the very words of Jesus? That is not the point at all. The radical critic, who is inclined to doubt whether any story about Jesus happened exactly as it is told, may find all manner of difficulties in other people's cherished beliefs; but about the 'wet and weedy' moralistic Jesus there is no need to doubt: he simply is not there. Whatever we believe the Lord of the Christian faith to have been like, he must have been extremely unlike a plaster saint.[5] Christian theology and Christian morality take their rise from a lively and vigorous teacher who enjoyed the good things of life, who was fascinating, good company, unexpected and inclined to turn people's fixed ideas upside down. These facts stand out, and are satisfyingly compatible with his strange, almost uncanny, authority.[6] There were times when his disciples were seized with awe as they followed him.[7] What fails to fit is the picture of the moralistic, shockable, goody-goody Jesus, so well-known and so easily outgrown.

Faith into creeds

Young Christians have been told that Jesus is an 'example' to us. Even if they are convinced they are not necessarily inspired. People who set good examples are seldom life-enhancing. There is another sense of 'example' which may be more encouraging: an example is an illustration. Christians can say, simply but not too simply, that the story of Jesus is an illustration, a picture, of God in action. Difficult ideas are best explained with examples. The idea that God does act in the world is difficult. It is best explained by showing a life in which we believe God did act. For Christians, the coming of Christ is an instance, indeed the instance, of what 'God acted' means.

If indeed belief in Christ does make sense of the world, both in theory and in practice, it does not have to be simple to understand or explain, even for grown-ups: any more than the physics and chemistry which make sense of the material world are easy to understand or explain. Most of us happily digest our dinners with no comprehension of enzymes. Truths which are too difficult for people to comprehend can underlie their lives: foundations not frills.

Human beings are so made that they want to find things out. To begin to understand more, there is no need to be a mature person already. On the contrary, trying to understand is a way of growing towards maturity. At best, understanding develops as a co-operative enterprise.

Unfortunately the doctrine that Jesus Christ was and is God the Son was worked out in polemics and strife, with curses and anathemas.[8] Twentieth-century people like to think they know better: or maybe they mind less whether their beliefs are inconsistent and their worship idolatrous. If they teach their children to pray to Jesus, they may not feel obliged to work out the implications of treating a human being as divine. They hope to manage all right without needing to have an answer ready for difficulties like, 'But I thought there was only one God' or 'Was he a real man, or just God pretending?' The creeds were developed as definitive answers to these fair questions.

Many would-be followers of Christ today look back on church history and shudder at the intolerance and cruelty of those battles long ago. They feel free to distance themselves from the finicky distinctions of the Church Fathers. They repudiate the bitterness, and they cheerfully decide that these arguments were not only ferocious but also pointless.

Sophisticated people are more inclined than naive people to complain that the formula 'perfect God, and perfect man' is unintelligible. As Dorothy L. Sayers only too neatly put it, 'The Father incomprehensible, the Son incomprehensible, the whole thing incomprehensible'.[9] To help new Christians to see the point of the old creeds comes to look like a low priority. Children ought to know about Jesus, to honour him as a holy man, sing songs about him and maybe say prayers to him; but to try to fit their ideas about him together into one picture is 'theology' and theology is not expected to be any practical use for young people growing up in the twentieth century.

The arguments go on. Some radicals would like to rewrite Christian doctrine to bring it up-to-date, conservatives doggedly defend it, and a good many people are happy not to bother but simply assume that traditional Christianity is hopelessly old-fashioned. Does it matter whether Jesus Christ is God the Son, or a good example, or a failed prophet? It does matter whether the people who have put their faith in him for nearly twenty centuries were fundamentally right in their trust. The effort to understand and decide is worthwhile. But the difficulty must not be under-estimated. The tares and wheat in our tradition are too 'compactly grown'[10] for us to separate. The load the uncharitable past hangs round the necks of Christians today is not easily shrugged off.

An optional extra?

There is one particularly respectable reason why liberal-minded Christians are so reluctant to teach distinctive Christianity. They have learnt to respect the believers in other faiths who are nowadays well represented among us, and who seem to care more for their religion than most Christians do. When children sit next to each other at school, their elders hesitate to sow dissension among them by controversial affirmations that Jesus is God as well as man.

Liberals perceive the 'two natures' doctrine as a barrier between Christianity and other faiths. So indeed it is. Robust traditionalists reply, 'So much the worse for the other faiths. Truth is truth. Where we differ somebody must be wrong, though of course we try to say so politely. How can they respect us if we lose our integrity?'

The argument is often fruitless, for the usual reason that the two sides are not listening to each other. Those of us who come down eventually on the orthodox side must understand that for radicals too this is a question of integrity. Radicals have come to interpret the Christian past as a mainly shocking story of intolerance and triumphalism, interspersed with patronizing condescension. The truth they see is the urgency of making amends. Christian distinctiveness from their point of view looks like a temptation to overcome. Conservatives will naturally be disturbed, but radicals are not too worried about teasing conservatives and upsetting a few apple-carts. The forbidden fruit of heresy has its attractions for people who are brave about knowing good and evil.[11]

The idea which may surprise the traditionalists is that Christian radicals characteristically have a strong secure faith in God underneath their superficial irreverence. It is from a basis of conviction that they dare to question established ideas. That is how they can be so strong-minded about facing difficulties. When they find the creeds are creating difficulties for them, they say so. It is loyal, not treacherous, to stand on what one does believe and be honest about one's doubts. Thinking conservatives may reasonably reply that radicals are being unduly defeatist about the tradition; but first they should recognize that defeatism need not imply disloyalty.

Radical Christians are strongly aware that some people who find the Christian creeds a stumbling block are more spiritual than some conventional Christians. It is embarrassing, as well as counter-productive, to brush aside their sincere faith. If the dogma that Jesus Christ was both God and man turns out to be a hindrance, it can seem tempting to treat it as expendable on the basis of a shared belief in God.

A lot depends on where one starts. Some begin by taking belief in God more or less for granted. On that basis, belief in Christ can seem like an optional extra. To stop insisting that Christ is God can look like Christian charity, in contrast with awkward conservatism. If fellow-believers are happy to venerate Jesus as a good and holy man, is it not an unnecessary complication to insist that he had 'two natures', that he was both divine and human? So the creeds come to look like something Christians are obliged to recite, not part of real life, certainly not something important to try to explain to children.

But dogma looks quite different when it makes sense of belief in God. There are many people in the late twentieth century who find the first step the hardest. They can hardly start with a shared faith, because in a seemingly secular universe God seems to have disappeared. The most promising approach to their particular problem is that God can be found in the life, death and resurrection of Jesus. If they are taught to belittle this conviction, what they lose is the cornerstone of faith, not a detail.

For some Christians, faith in Jesus Christ answers the questions they find they have to ask, and brings belief in God to earth. They say that he is the way, the truth and the life,[12] not to keep others out but to keep themselves in. Their neighbour may be a liberal, or perhaps a Muslim, who honours Jesus as holy and inspired. They naturally want to ask, like Peter at the end of the Fourth Gospel asking what would happen to John,[13] 'Lord, what about this man?' The reply given to Peter is, 'What is that to you? Follow me!'

Questions and answers

Formulae come to life when people find out how to use them to solve puzzling problems. The way to make sense of the idea that Jesus Christ is man and God is to ask, once again,[14] *To what questions is it the answer?* Wittgenstein gave a piece of advice, 'Don't ask for the meaning, ask for the use.'[15] Philosophers have been saying this to each other ever since, because they have found that this maxim is, indeed, useful. It is not a shallow suggestion that mere 'utility' is enough without looking deeper. 'Ask for the use' suggests that when we are confronted by a way of speaking which seems abstract or obscure, we should find out what work it does for people who speak in this way. What problems can this language solve?

The formula that Jesus Christ is God and man was worked out to answer different questions from ours. The first followers of Jesus, who had become witnesses to his rising from the dead, found that he had stretched their whole way of thinking and speaking. They were impelled to proclaim him as more than a good and holy teacher, more than a healer, more than another prophet. They were convinced that as well as being in heaven he was present in their lives: that this particular human being was worthy not only of their admiration, but of their worship. Believing in one God, they began in good conscience to give Jesus divine names, Lord, Son, Logos. Sooner or later they would have to answer questions like, 'Are you idolaters?' 'Have you given up the belief that God is One?' The answer they developed was the doctrine that God had taken human flesh. It was no abstract exercise to struggle with what that doctrine could mean.

Today Christian preachers have to start further back. They cannot assume that faith in God at least is straightforward and shared by most people. Fundamental belief in God as Creator and Sustainer of the world seemed obvious once, but has become controversial now that the physical and biological sciences have colonized the universe. The onus has been shifted on to religious people to make room for God in the whole picture.[16] There used to be just a few recalcitrant free-thinkers who dared to cast doubt on the existence of God. Today anyone who has learnt some science at school may want to know, 'Do you have any evidence for this idea of yours that God's presence really can be found?' Indeed, it is too optimistic to say that people want to know. Quite often the negative answer is taken for granted and the question is hardly asked.

Believers must face the fact that they may not gain a hearing. It is not difficult to dismiss belief in God. 'All this is wishful thinking. It hasn't enough foundation to be worth taking seriously. If God were real, God would put in a more definite appearance.' Christians assert that God has done just that.

They still ought not to add 'Q.E.D.'[17] Would-be clinching arguments impress without convincing. Debating points squash opposition without providing illumination. If the audience see the rabbit put into the hat they will not be impressed when it comes out again. 'This man is divine' could never prove 'God exists'.

'God was made man' is an affirmation which makes belief in God more convincing, not a proof that God exists. Belief in Jesus can bring belief in God to earth: but taking Jesus for granted begs as many questions as taking God for granted. The first Christians enlarged their faith in God to include faith in Jesus. They did not make faith in Jesus a substitute for faith in God.

Though in various Christian hymns Christians sing about Christ as foundation, the image of a keystone or a cornerstone[18] can be used more exactly and more vividly. Jesus Christ fits into place to hold our incomplete faith up. Keystones and cornerstones do not underlie the building but bond together a structure that is already taking shape. The Christian hope is that our Creator comes to our rescue: and these ideas of making and saving reinforce each other.

The less mature the enquirers are, the worse it is to think that slipshod arguments will do. Telling unwary people, children or grown-ups, that assertions are certainties is unfair; and also counter-productive. Plenty of inexperienced people, children and grown-ups, are quite wary enough to be simply sceptical. Nobody, trustful or canny, is going to be enlightened in that way. At all ages, people deserve careful statements used carefully.

The affirmation that Jesus was 'God's entry into human life'[19] need not be offered as a proof. Its role is more subtle and complex: to start explaining what believers are talking about, and to disprove, or at least undermine, the disproofs.[20] There is not much point in arguing with people who are not ready to hear. They will hardly be convinced 'though one rose from the dead'.[21] Removing obstacles to belief may be more to the purpose than providing evidence.

If believers could accept the fact that a good deal of the argument is going on in their own minds, they might be less discouraged. They keep hearing a little voice whispering in their ears: 'They say you don't know what you are talking about. *Do you know what you are talking about?* What difference does belief in God make to anything? What on earth can you say to the children if they start asking whether God is really real?'

The little voice needs honest attention before anyone else, young or old, can be convinced. The statement that 'God was in Christ'[22] is for people who have some idea of God. It can begin to explain how they can go on being believers, in the face of today's difficulties. It can fill this role for them, just because it was not thought up as special pleading when the questions became pressing, but was already in place as the foundation of the Christian creeds.

5

Finding God in Creation

On what grounds do you call millions of light-years of inter-galactic space a 'waste'? A waste of what? Of space?

John Austin Baker[1]

Maker of heaven and earth

The distinctive Christian belief in Jesus Christ, God living a human life, is rooted in the basic religious belief in God, the Creator and Sustainer of the universe. Have we any idea what we are talking about when we say that God is maker of heaven and earth, responsible for everything? Unless theology is coherently related to science, our whole understanding of the world will be broken-backed. If children's scripture lessons and physics lessons seem incompatible, it is not too hard to guess which version of the truth they will leave behind when they try to bring all their beliefs into focus.

For twentieth-century Christians, the idea that the universe began with a sudden enormous explosion looks like a specially theological bit of physics. It is congenial, perhaps dangerously congenial, to say, 'In the beginning was the Big Bang.' It is easy to imagine that God set it off, like igniting a well-controlled firework, at which we all say 'Ooh – aah'. Just when science was threatening to have no need for the hypothesis of God,[2] the concept of the Big Bang offers to make room for creation after all.

The ending of Stephen Hawkings' *A Brief History of Time* is famous: 'We shall know the mind of God.'[3] Is a physicist nearer to God by comprehending the Big Bang? The answer is No, if he is thinking in terms of proofs, but Yes, if he is thinking in terms of understanding. Likewise a biologist is nearer to God by understanding evolution; and an anatomist is nearer to God by understanding the structure of the human body. For anyone who is willing to entertain the idea that the universe is God's creation, to study any part of the universe is to study God's handiwork, and to study it reverently can be to draw nearer to God.

Most of us cannot approach God by means of astrophysics. For most of us, it would be pretentious to the point of hypocrisy to push our way into the scientific debate. If we use the idea of the Big Bang we must realize that what we say is probably baby-talk. It may be none the worse for that, so long as we know what we are doing. Baby-talk is good for communicating with babies, and many of us are not as adult as we like to think, particularly not in relation to God.

Picture language

Christians are accustomed to the 'baby-talk' about how the universe began which comes at the beginning of the Bible. Because Genesis both comes first and means 'origin', Christians have a strong impression that the creation stories are the foundation of their faith. Jews, reading the same scriptures, build their faith upon the creation of the people of God. Their foundation stories are God's promise to Abraham, and especially God's great rescue of the children of Israel from Egypt.

Jews and Christians alike believe that these ancient traditions do indeed answer to reality. God is the maker of heaven and earth, and God did enter into human history by choosing a particular people. The chosen people passed on the story of their origins from generation to generation. Nobody can be sure now what the historical facts were around which the legends grew, but those who still stand in that tradition believe that what emerges is the truth: 'The Lord our God is one Lord.'[4]

When God's people began to reflect about how the world itself came to be, it was in poetry that they described how before history, or rather, underlying history, everything has its origin in God's word. When children are introduced to the Bible they need to be told that the stories at the beginning of the Book of Genesis are inspired poetry. To treat them as the first chapter of world history is needless confusion. To set them in opposition to scientific accounts is mistaken loyalty.

Myths serve human beings well for talking about realities beyond our understanding. If nowadays we are able to say more, not less, about the course of nature, so much the better. To translate the opening words of Genesis, 'In the beginning God created the heavens and the earth' into the language of the Big Bang can be a good way to show twentieth-century people, including children, that 'God said, Let there be light' is not the only way of telling how the world began.

Is poetry still valid as a way of understanding? It cannot be a rival, simpler kind of physics: so are poems just incantations? Is anything left of 'I will consider the heavens, even the work of thy fingers: the moon and the stars, which thou has ordained,'[5] if we do not suppose that God has fingers? What remains is a way of putting into words the wonder at God's creation which prose cannot express.

God's handiwork

A physicist can feel wonder. The manipulative scientist without a heart or a soul, for whom the universe is machinery, is a stereotype of fiction. On the contrary, scientists who study realities which cannot be seen or touched are well placed to lead the way out of today's notorious shallow materialism.[6] The things that scientists want to say about the physical universe are becoming stranger and less mechanical, and so it is becoming respectable to take seriously the things religious people want to say about God. Since scientists give the lead, it seems to be in order once again for intelligent people to believe in paradoxical realities. Religion is allowed its say.

It may look as if our age is characterized most of all by a denial of spirit.[7] Sensitive human beings feel hemmed in by people who seem happy to think of life as no different from matter, who appear to live comfortably without needing to feel any reverence. When it turns out that matter itself does not consist of plain lumps of inert stuff, mechanistic ideas become a lot less plausible.

Reverence finds a foothold again, not in spite of the scientists but encouraged by them.

Physicists arrive, marvelling, at austere mathematical equations. Embryologists study the beginnings of individual existence and are struck with awe at the tiny living beings in their test-tubes. Biologists and ethologists find the variety and complexity of creatures, leading their lives without regard for human convenience, more wonderful than a pre-Darwinian menagerie. It is not a long step to, 'O Lord, how manifold are thy works: in wisdom hast thou made them all; the earth is full of thy riches.'[8]

The grandeur of the universe is not mine and most of it is quite alien to me. There is no need to live in the country, still less to be a nature mystic, to be capable of attending, with wonder, to things which human beings have not made. Any of us can be awestruck by the immensity of the sky, or by the potential to grow into a large plant which is packed up in a small seed, or by the fact that half the surface of the earth is sea, 'wherein are things creeping innumerable, both small and great beasts,'[9] which will never be seen by human eyes. Wonder is a kind of contemplation even if God is not named.

Looking at nature is a way to practice attending and to learn how to appreciate: from children bringing strange odds and ends to the playgroup nature table, to an old lady cherishing an African violet. Iris Murdoch said, 'we take a self-forgetful pleasure in the sheer alien pointless independent existence of animals, birds, stones and trees.' She went on:

> It is so patently a good thing to take delight in flowers and animals that people who bring home potted plants and watch kestrels might even be surprised at the notion that these things have anything to do with virtue.[10]

Attending carefully to something other than *me* does, indeed, 'take me out of myself'. In the light of Iris Murdoch's austerity, the next step has to be trodden gingerly. Can nature take me out of myself, into praise? If nature is God's handiwork, unselfconscious attention to nature becomes what Christians may call a 'means of grace'. The austerity has to remain, to guard against presumption. God's creation is not to be domesticated. Attending to nature means taking nature as it comes, 'alien', 'pointless' and 'independent', not at all adapted to our needs, claiming appreciation in its own right. St Augustine said something similar long ago: 'It is the nature of things considered in itself, without regard for our convenience or inconvenience, that gives glory to the Creator.'[11]

One way of becoming as little children[12] is to expect the world to be full of wonders. A small boy woke up his grandparents one morning with the request, one might say demand, 'Show me things.' Addressed to God as a prayer, that could make a change from 'Give me things.' 'Thou shalt show us wonderful things in thy righteousness, O God of our salvation . . . thou that makest the outgoings of the morning and evening to praise thee.'[13]

In Thomas Traherne's almost mystical perception, what God shows us, God gives us. To appreciate what God has made, without grabbing, is to be given it as our very own. 'Appreciate' is a timid word compared with Traherne's word 'enjoy'. His unpossessive enjoyment of God's creation made everything a gift of God:

> You never Enjoy the World aright, till the Sea itself floweth in your Veins, till you are Clothed with the Heavens, and Crowned with the Stars: and Perceiv your self to be the Sole Heir of the whole World: and more then so, becaus Men are in it who are evry one Sole Heirs, as well as you. Till you can Sing and Rejoyce and delight in God, as Misers do in Gold, and Kings in Scepters, you never enjoy the World.[14]

More sedately, Joseph Addison celebrated the glory of God in God's works:

> The spacious firmament on high
> With all the blue ethereal sky,
> And spangled heavens, a shining frame,
> Their great Original proclaim:
> The unwearied sun, from day to day,
> Does his Creator's power display,
> And publishes to every land
> The work of an almighty hand.

Soon as the evening shades prevail,
The moon takes up the wondrous tale,
And nightly to the listening earth
Repeats the story of her birth:
While all the stars that round her burn,
And all the planets in their turn,
Confirm the tidings as they roll,
And spread the truth from pole to pole.

Traherne is politely called a mystic. Addison is accused of being a 'deist', because he has not put in the Christian gospel. They are not so far apart. They are converging, from different directions, upon the glory of God the Creator: attending to the natural world and praising God for what they find.[15] Addison's eighteenth-century reasonableness is not some kind of disqualification. The heavenly bodies are not providing a sub-Christian 'proof of the existence of God'. They are glorifying their maker:

What though in solemn silence all
Move round the dark terrestrial ball?
What though no real voice nor sound
Amid their radiant orbs be found?
In reason's ear they all rejoice,
And utter forth a glorious voice,
For ever singing as they shine,
'The hand that made us is divine.'

Both Traherne and Addison could agree with St Augustine: 'I asked the whole frame of earth about my God, and it answered, 'I am not he, but he made me.'[16]

No point?

What has happened to Iris Murdoch's 'pointlessness', if the point of creation is to glorify God? The point of pointlessness, we might paradoxically say, is that creation does not have to be *useful*. The starry heavens are not 'for' anything. They are for their own sake: or rather, for God's sake, for God's delight. Why should God be expected to think on a small scale, and put us in a universe which would hold only us human beings, some animals for us to rule over, a certain amount of wilderness for us to tame, some mountains to climb because they are there, and not much more? Nature is not a backdrop. The poet who wrote Psalm 104 inhabited what seemed a smaller universe than ours, but he knew that Leviathan lived in the deep sea 'to take his pastime therein',[17] maybe to amuse God:[18] but not to feed, serve, or even console human beings.

Christians might learn from Iris Murdoch to think more spaciously. People who try to be good are easily caught by petty dilemmas. 'Everything must be useful *or* useless' is like 'everything must be permitted *or* forbidden.' God is easily pictured as a great bureaucrat who grants certificates of world-worthiness, instead of a Creator whose works are excellent for their own sake, or a Father who delights in the children's company here and now.

People who require everything to lead to something else are at the mercy of the terrifying notion that once their aims are achieved there will be nothing to hope for.[19] For many Christians today, the idea of heaven has gone dead. In heaven nothing can be useful any more, because our work will be done, and all that remains will be an 'endless Sabbath'. Leisure, nothing to do, has plenty of point as an earthly treat, when it makes a lovely change from far too much to do; but everlasting leisure has the futility of unemployment.[20] Surely in heaven we shall long for the rewarding rhythm of work, rest and work again, to which we were trained on earth? When grown-ups imagine heaven as mostly just standing about,[21] it is no wonder that children find the whole idea far from encouraging, and grow up doing their best to forget about the Christian hope.

Perhaps, contrariwise, naive children can be an encouragement to sophisticated grown-ups. Children are generally not much concerned with usefulness. When they are not obliged to work they do not rest, they play. If the kingdom of heaven belongs to such as these,[22] maybe after all the best rehearsals for heaven in this life are not strenuous efforts for worthy purposes, which are bound to come to an end, but unselfconscious enjoyments and lighthearted celebrations.

The world around us

Celebration of the 'alien pointless independent existence' of God's creatures is more than a sort of pretty icing on a pious cake. Human beings are becoming belatedly aware that they have horribly taken nature for granted. Appreciation of God's universe can be just the corrective we need, not only for heedless damage but for despairing recklessness.

Children, and grown-ups, are taught nowadays how badly humanity has behaved. 'Man' is the top creature, the king of the universe, but unfortunately the species that is called the crown of creation is supreme, not sublime. Feminists too can say 'man' here. Many secular sermons are preached, in which religion is blamed for setting up the notion of 'man's dominion'. In response, among some Christians, a kind of unanswerable but not responsible breast-beating goes on. 'We' must be wrong: but 'we' really means 'you lot who have not yet seen the light'.

The gospel, or rather, the bad news, of the environment is sometimes proclaimed almost to saturation point. People who are only too willing to believe that if something is good for you then it must be unpleasant make a reversal which is no happier, and believe that if something is unpleasant then it must be good for you. Suddenly we are required to feel guilty about hitherto harmless comforts, like having machines to work for us. Looking after the natural world becomes a matter of an impossible and dismal duty to which most of us are quite unequal.

Weariness begins when moralists nag. People refuse to amend their ways, from selfishness of course, but also because they feel helpless and hopeless. Once they could have gone by bus and saved fuel, but now that everyone has a car the buses have disappeared. Is it a Christian duty for people who are too old to take to bicycles to become immobile, cut off from their families and friends? The more people are blamed for consumerism, the more trapped they feel, and the more they become defensive and even aggressive. It is paradoxical to say that encouragement is what they need, but in a way it is: not encouragement to damage the world around us, but encouragement to see the world differently.[23]

To begin to see anything differently, most of us need to be shown. If God does show people things, it is generally by way of other people. The strength of the green movement is not the tendency of the enlightened few to moralize about 'the environment', which may sound like a dreary abstraction, but the contagious enthusiasm of people who look with understanding at the world around them in its particular detail, and will show it to the rest of us if only we will look. Television programmes, conservation zoos, friends who watch birds, gardeners, painters, poets: all these are able to open other people's eyes to the specific glories of creation. Once enough people begin to mind, they find ways to act.

Maker of makers

We understand now that humanity is part of nature, not separate from nature. This is all the more reason for celebrating humanity. Christians who indulge in undiscriminating self-abasement are not glorifying their Creator. It must be counter-productive to keep on denigrating our own species. Human beings are animals: not 'only' animals but special animals,[24] among the glories of creation; and perhaps after all its crown.

If we are truly looking at the creation to see what it is really like, not making assumptions about what it must be like, we must particularly look at the creatures we ourselves are. There is no need to be so defeatist as to say that the only thing special about human beings is our special destructiveness. The worst is the corruption of the best: we also are especially creative.

Here, if we like, is a refreshed meaning for the ancient idea that humanity is made in the 'image of God'.[25] If we look on creatures as God's handiwork, we can say that human beings are made with a wider scope: these creatures are themselves creators. Whatever else we may be, we are made to be makers. We can take part consciously in our own making; we certainly make one another; and most characteristically we make *things*, simple, intricate, useful, dangerous, convenient, beautiful.

Creation myths, including our own,[26] picture God as starting with chaos and creating order. When God's creatures are able to do that they are indeed godlike. Philosophically-minded theologians have found it desirable to improve upon this mythical way of thinking about creation, because they are not satisfied with the idea that God had anything already there to work on. They feel responsible for distinguishing God absolutely from creatures. Their formulation is that God the Creator needs no raw material at all. God made everything 'out of nothing'. Human creation, which rearranges what is there already, is different in kind, though still godlike. The story-tellers and the philosophers can agree that human makers put their God-given creativity to work to shape their God-given raw material.

'Creativity' can mean high flights of genius, but it has plenty of ordinary forms. People cook meals, plant flowers, furnish rooms, draw pictures, sing songs, tell stories. They put their hearts into all manner of skills like these, they find them satisfying, and they teach them to their children.

After thousands of years of human history almost everything most human beings see when they look around them was formed, recently or long ago, by other human beings.[27] Landscape is 'nature'; but in developed countries most landscape is also an artifact, like townscape. If we attend to the countryside and praise God for it, we are praising the Creator of the people who created the fields and hedges. If we listen to music or look at pictures we may proceed to praise God as the Creator of the world in which genius comes to be. There are, so to say, two layers of creation here.

Creativeness does not raise human beings above nature. We differ from other animals in degree, not absolutely. In particular, like other animals, we are fruitful and multiply. Procreation is pro-creation: a kind of making on God's behalf. Living creatures give one another existence, and some of them bring each other up as well. They set their mark upon the physical world, digging holes and making nests, sometimes of great complexity and elegance. It is not only human beings who create things which are more beautiful than they need to be for their purpose, though as far as we know it is only human beings who can celebrate beauty.

Most characteristic of human beings is the use of language. Animals communicate with one another, so again we have a difference of degree not of kind; but for human beings language is more than a way of imparting immediate information. We use language to show one another things, far away as well as near, delightful as well as useful, theoretical as well as practical. Besides using words to describe and explain the world, we can shape words themselves into marvellous things in their own right for showing to one another. It is no wonder that poets used to be called 'makers'. With words we can give each other the world, and make new imaginary worlds to give.

Creation, often, is a joint enterprise. Composers need performers, architects need builders, dramatists need actors, and writers are not independent of publishers. But there is another more surprising kind of joint enterprise, the creative co-operation between the maker of the work and the listeners or lookers who receive and respond to it. Sir Ernst Gombrich in *Art and Illusion*[28] pointed out how we miss a lot if we take for granted that some pictures show nature 'just as it is'. For example, Constable's 'Wivenhoe Park' is by no means a 'transcript of nature'. Even a photograph is not that.[29] The artist's work is not simple making, but a 'complex process of interaction between making and matching, suggesting and projection'.[30] Children are doing something like this when they 'make trains' out of 'red, green and yellow blocks, all in a row with one double on top'[31] and push them along saying 'choo choo'. Cartoonists and illustrators show us individual faces in sketchy lines.[32] Delightfully, there are far more art-forms than we may have realized.

Sometimes an artist 'gives the beholder increasingly "more to do", he draws him into the magic circle of creation and allows him to experience something of the thrill of "making".'[33] In any case the beholder does not start from scratch, but draws on quantities of experience and expectations, from life and from other works of art, to help or hinder in 'seeing something' in this particular one. The showing and seeing is a shared enterprise between them, building on what the beholder brings as well as on what the artist has made.

Can we go on to say that how we behold God's creation, and what we make of it, is a shared enterprise between ourselves, other people and God? Human beings who show one another things[34] may be as unsophisticated as children playing trains, as witty as Osbert Lancaster, as inspired as Raphael, as revolutionary as Picasso. Artists of all kinds, and the people whose experience is enriched by what they have made, can share, consciously or unconsciously, in the inventiveness of God the Creator. The common factor in this enterprise is not strenuous effort to find profound messages hidden in works of art, but hopeful looking to make out what is there to be seen.

6

Finding God in Providence?

The lions roaring after their prey do seek their meat from God.

Ps. 104.21

The rough and the smooth

Does this happy picture of people enjoying the world, appreciating each other's work in it, and praising God, do justice to how terrible the world can be? There is much more to life than artistic appreciation, and a great deal of the 'more' is horrifying. It must be trivial to imagine God as a sort of entertainer at a children's party, putting on a show to amuse us all, with plenty of audience participation. It is high time to remember the huge But confronting every cheerful picture of the universe. In the natural world around us, as in the events of our human lives, there is plenty to deplore as well as plenty to admire and enjoy. People who talk about creation must take the rough with the smooth.

If there is a God who is maker of heaven and earth, God is responsible for everything in heaven and earth: for earthquakes and viruses and human weakness, as well as for flowers and sunsets and human love. God's responsibility is at the heart of the ancient problem of evil. Preachers tend to make a sideways move and say rather quickly: 'What really matters is not evil but sin'; and people who want to be convinced hastily agree. What could be worse than doing what we know to be wrong? Volcanoes do not flout God's love. Cats torment mice in all innocence. But we human beings, who ought to know better, sin against the light.

We ought to know better than to use arguments like that, and smother people's perplexity with imputed guilt. Of course a liar is more wicked than a tumour, because a tumour is not wicked at all. But God's responsibility for making this mixed world

47

includes the responsibility for allowing liars and tumours to have their place in it.

'It's *all* our fault' cannot be the whole answer. Human sinfulness is no more infinite than human virtue. Children who are quite often naughty, and who do not doubt that grown-ups know best, are helpless to deny that bad behaviour causes a lot of trouble and that God has the right to be angry. But as they grow up a good many of them will feel the injustice of always blaming human beings and always praising God.

In the end the answer must somehow include, 'It will turn out to have been worth while.' Believers need not be ashamed of their firm conviction that God is in charge and that God can be trusted. They already find many signs of the world's worthwhileness: past encouragement, present clues and foretastes for the future. Optimism is more lovable, and more constructive, than pessimism. Often we get what we look for. Surely it is a sign of grace to look out for good rather than evil and to trust that God's love will prevail in the end over everything that threatens us? Indeed it is; but Christian optimism should be responsibly grounded.

When believers take the trouble to ask questions about the basis of their faith, about where in the world they find their God, many hopeful answers suggest themselves. Can God be found in Christ? – in nature? – in providence? – in conscience? – in church? – in the Bible? – in other people? – in things? The answer is Yes: but the most doubtful of these is providence.

Expectations

Faith in God is generally supposed to be faith in providence. The next move has to be sceptical: not as a permanent policy, but as a temporary check. It must be said that providential control of everyday events is not the most promising place to start looking for the grace of God. It is untrue and often cruel to give the impression that people can forget all the difficult dogmas and fall back on faith in God's providential care as if that were straightforward.

To cast doubt on belief in providence is a heavy responsibility. 'Tread softly, because you tread on my dreams.'[1] Many people have a strong faith in God as their loving Father who looks after them in all the changing scenes of life. They find God among the pots and pans, in the factory, the office, the hospital ward, the garden, and the street, as well as in the fields and the hills. They talk to God, they ask for what they need, and they believe that God responds to their prayers. Sometimes they find that God says Wait or even No, but often with humble gratitude they feel themselves directly aware of guidance and blessings. This is how they experience God's grace. 'I waited patiently for the Lord, and he inclined unto me, and heard my calling.'² How can fellow believers whose faith is weaker presume to criticize?

People who walk with God find cause for gratitude in all circumstances. Their state is literally the more gracious: unless they begin to take it for granted. Presumption can be innocently naive. Emmy in *Vanity Fair* exclaimed, 'Poor Becky, poor Becky! How thankful, how thankful I ought to be'; and Thackeray added, 'I doubt whether that practice of piety inculcated upon us by our womankind in early youth, namely, to be thankful because we are better off than somebody else, be a very rational religious exercise.'³

Being grateful to God for good fortune begins to go wrong if there is a lurking idea that the people who are not so blessed are somehow or other less dear to God. Gratitude slips easily into smugness. 'The heart is deceitful above all things, and desperately wicked.'⁴ That is a strong way of pointing out that human virtue is particularly prone to topple over into self-deception. Good people begin to take themselves too seriously and nobody is brave enough, or unkind enough, to argue or mock them out of it.

To undermine somebody else's confidence is a failure of charity. When people are bearing witness to what they themselves have found to make them grateful they should be heard, not snubbed. But also, people must be allowed and encouraged to be honest about what they have not found. Christians ought not to let themselves slip into the kind of mechanical thankfulness which invites the reaction, 'You would say that whatever happened.'

There are difficulties in theory and in practice about the notion of God continually intervening in response to faithful prayers.

Christians who keep looking out for everyday providences do not know what they ask. Unless God the Creator relinquished that kind of close control, the physical world would have to be very different from the dependable reality it is. Alice discovered in Wonderland that you need a hard mallet for playing croquet, not a live flamingo.[5]

Trust in providence is easily trivialized. 'Please, Lord, send us a fine day for the church fête.' Simple favouritism would hardly be worthy of God. Most of us have outgrown, 'Please let our team win.' It is harder to outgrow the traffic jam prayer, '*Please* let me get there in time'; but in a cool hour we know that if the lights have all turned green for us we have been lucky, not holy. It is said that 'the devil looks after his own'; but God, in that straightforward sense, evidently does not. People who think they are meant to have a helpline to heaven often have discouraging difficulties in getting through. Even if it were right for the world to be run for the benefit of the devout, the world is not run for the benefit of the devout.

A small aircraft crashes on a motorway, hitting two cars. Nobody is dangerously hurt and someone remarks, 'God must have been looking after them.' The next day a bomb explodes in Florence, killing a whole family. Whatever place can be found for this in God's ultimate purpose, it would be monstrous to suggest that God was too busy looking after some of the greatest pictures in the world to protect the human beings. It is more seemly, and more consistent with Christian faith, to reserve judgment about these emergencies and put them alongside the deaths of 'those eighteen upon whom the tower in Siloam fell and killed them,'[6] for which the Lord had no easy explanation to give.

The main reason for being cautious about identifying providence everywhere is that the examples believers so gladly give of little providences are insensitive, in the light of other believers' sorrowful experience of their heartfelt prayers seemingly remaining unanswered. People ask God for protection against danger; they beg for healing and health; and God gives no sign.

Death, premature and pointless, does not belong only to bad old days. 'That strong unmerciful tyrand' still

Takis, on the motheris breast sowkand,
The babe full of benignitie.[7]

Cancer overcomes good Christians in the prime of their usefulness. Earthquakes are not caused by human folly or sin. The
assumption that God must have done this and can be expected to
do that is a stumbling block, not an encouragement, and may be a
way of taking the name of the Lord in vain.

Chosen people

It would be perverse to deny that the Bible, Hebrew and
Christian, is full of belief in providence. Just so: the biblical
writers are indeed bearing witness to what they themselves have
found. What they tell is what they have experienced. The story is
complex but the gist of it is that the God of Abraham, Isaac and
Jacob is a faithful God, who sets particular individuals particular
tasks, who has led the people out of Egypt, made a Covenant with
them, given them a Law to live by, borne with their backslidings
and constantly intervened to save them: decisively, Christians
say, in Jesus Christ.

What God decides to do is characteristically different from
what human beings expect. God is not to be stereotyped. To take
God's policies for granted cannot be the right way to show
faithful trust. It is tempting to play safe, acknowledge God's
blessings of old, and simply stop looking for providence except in
the past. Is it good enough to recognize and declare God's long-
ago mercies to the Chosen People, and put aside assurances for
individuals in the present and the future?

At least believers should be in less of a hurry to explain all
everyday happenings in terms of divine care. It is all very well to
say, 'I have been young, and now am old: and yet saw I never the
righteous forsaken',[8] but such sunny optimism is not borne out in
general by human life, by the biblical record, nor by the
experience of the Lord himself.[9] St Augustine was perplexed by
this psalm. He feared, not without reason, that someone might
'be inwardly scandalized, and ask, "Is what I have chanted really
true? . . . the Scriptures play us false".'[10]

Yet defeatisim about God's care for us will not do either. Though 'proof-texts' are out of fashion, the whole impact of biblical teaching ought to matter to us. Even more plainly than the story of the children of Israel, Christian scriptures seem to encourage belief in special providences. Whatever criticisms Jesus made of traditional piety, surely the psalmists' trustfulness was congenial to him? However much we try to argue, did he not teach that the heavenly Father would provide individually for each one of us?

Asking

On the face of it the Gospels appear to say, after all, that disciples of Jesus can abandon fretfulness for the simple reason that there will be nothing to give them any cause to fret. 'All things are possible with God.'[11] Christians are to ask and they will receive.[12] They are not to worry about food or clothes or anything else, but peacefully have faith in their heavenly Father, who will not give his children a stone when they ask for bread.[13] 'If God so clothe the grass of the field, which today is alive and tomorrow is cast into the oven, will he not much more clothe you, O men of little faith?'[14] What could be plainer? If the extravagance of this is toned down, is what Jesus taught restated, or rejected?

The message that God is longing to bless us comes through in all the Gospels. If the teaching is taken seriously, does it endorse expectations of everyday protection for faithful Christians? One way of making the sayings into 'proof-texts' in the bad sense is to wrench them out of context. The context of 'all things are possible with God' is not an illness with a bad prognosis nor an intractable worry, but the difficulty rich people have in entering the kingdom. God is able to save: not, God will run our lives for us.

But what about asking, every time we obediently use the Lord's Prayer, for our daily bread?[15] Surely that is literally and straightforwardly earthly: but Christians still suffer from famine. Using this petition can be daunting to faith. It looks like a clear case of unrealistic trust in God's providence, and yet it is a command of the Lord. It is tempting to detach 'bread' from physical food and give it a spiritual meaning. That would be cheating; but it is worth bearing in mind that the Greek word translated 'daily' is an unusual word,[16] which may point beyond ordinary housekeeping towards the heavenly feast in God's kingdom. To trust in God to give us tomorrow's bread need not always and only mean to feel confident about where the next meal is coming from.

The interconnections of material and spiritual blessings are complex and subtle, even in the Sermon on the Mount, still more when we include in the picture the whole story of the passion and resurrection. In the light of the cross, asking in the name of Jesus is something special.[17] It has never been a formula for securing a quiet life, still less for obtaining casual favours. To use the phrase, 'in the name of Jesus Christ' as a magic spell, or on the other hand to use it as a merely polite form of words to round off a prayer, is precisely to take the name of the Lord in vain. To ask in the name of Jesus should be to claim the privilege of joining in the prayers of Jesus himself, and of being included in whatever the upshot turns out to be.

Christians may hope that when they enter whole-heartedly into the purposes of the Lord they will understand more of what makes everything worthwhile and will find themselves enabled to make their own characteristic contributions. Their own particular wants will not be thwarted, though surely enlarged. If that sounds platitudinously pious, it can be likened to what happens in a good marriage. When husbands and wives act on behalf of each other, their identities are not submerged. They find out together what will make them both happy:

> Oh I must feel your brain prompt mine,
> Your heart anticipate my heart.[18]

Sceptics may suspect that some cheating is going on here. Are we still allowed to ask God in a straightforward way about our ordinary natural human wishes for ourselves and for one another, or are we not? Suppose a friend is ill. 'Please God, help!' means 'help her to get better', not 'help her to die a good death', nor even, in all honesty, 'Thy will be done'. 'The answer may be

No' is all very well, but the answer is No so often, with no explanation of either Yes or No to help us, that it can be hard to see how God can be like a loving father of a family. Is the heavenly Father only a sort of glorified Father Christmas after all, whose mail will have to be intercepted and answered by kindly grown-ups if the children are not to be disillusioned?

Prayer for one another depends upon the double conviction that God does bless and that somehow human prayer can make a difference. These can come together in the belief, 'God will let me help.' We are confident that we can help when it is a matter of doing something; so praying might be a way of joining in what God is doing, somewhat like earmarking a subscription. When we understand the whole course of our lives, we may be able to say 'That was my bit': not 'I persuaded God to do that after all.'

Everyday life gives good reason, and Hebrew and Christian scriptures give good authority, for refusing to presume upon special providences. Since we are responsible for one another, arousing unfounded hopes can be as much a failure of charity as discouraging cherished hopes. There is scope for being tentative, for looking at what the world is really like. When we look, we find a mixture: what matters is to get the emphasis right. The present argument is offered as a corrective to glibness, not as a counterblast to gratitude.

Troubles

The idea that if people are good they can expect God to arrange things for them needs correcting because it is unrealistic and therefore cruel. Simple faith does not have to be like that, neither the simple faith of Jesus nor simple faith in Jesus. It is false to suggest that God's children have only to say their prayers and Jesus will see that everything comes right. From the psalmists and prophets onwards, religious people have often had to understand that the world does not accommodate itself even to their pious hopes.

People who have taken providence for granted have found out the hard way that providence does not mean what they thought. When Christians find themselves and the whole universe 'groaning in travail',[19] it is more responsible to tell them to read the Book of Job than to tell them to rely on providence here and now. It was Job's comforters, not Job, who were convinced that his troubles were all for the best.

The doctrine of providential care which seems so suitable for children is insulting as soon as they come across real suffering. Many people are taught when they are young that everything that happens to them is the will of God. Then, when something goes wrong, besides their distress they have the extra problem of trying to see how a good God could possibly have wanted this. So they ask despairingly, 'How can I pray now?'

The obvious way not to ascribe miseries to God's will after all is to find some sinful human beings to blame. It is no wonder that people take up this alternative with alacrity. Unhappiness is all ready to become anger, shaping itself into bitterness against other people or helpless self-accusation. Justifying oneself and blaming oneself are two ways of manifesting the same state of mind. It seems as if the most natural question to ask in deep trouble is, 'What have I done to deserve this?'

The foundation for this reaction may have been laid in well-meaning distortions of Christian teaching. Religion is supposed to be very serious. When the grown-ups mention God, they tend to frown and say 'Hush'. Why are they so solemn, when they have set aside the cross as too gloomy for children, and the fear of God as too gloomy for anybody? The seriousness which ebbing Christian reverence is apt to leave behind, like a line of seaweed washed up on a beach, is the idea of a disapproving God, in whose sight we are always at fault, unlovable even though unpunished. This notion is the more insidious because it is not taught directly but picked up from grown-up attitudes. Then later on the troubles of life make people doubly unhappy, not only hurt but guilty.

To make matters worse, believers who suppose that God is not really on their side still feel bound to be truly grateful. We are taught to thank God for all our blessings. Does it follow that when something dreadful has happened we are to be thankful none the less? Ought we positively to be glad of trouble because we know it is God's plan? That is how 'Thy will be done' comes to seem dismally fatalistic.

Far from assuming that every situation reveals God's will and all we can ask for is grace to put up with it, 'Thy will be done' is a prayer which looks ahead when what is going to happen is still unsure and asks for the truly best outcome. The prayer even implies that God's will is *not* already done, that there is something to be prayed for. To pray 'Thy will be done' is a way of aligning ourselves with God's purposes. It is not meant to be said in a sad resigned way because things have already gone wrong and we have to believe this was God's doing. It was in the agonizing uncertainty of Gethsemane that we are told that Jesus prayed 'not what I will, but what thou wilt'.[20] There is a difference between saying, 'because I am suffering, that must be what God wants' and 'God's will be done, even if it requires suffering.'

When somebody else is in trouble it becomes particularly clear that God's will is not always done, yet, and that plenty of things that happen are against God's will. We need not think of God as positively sending people disappointments, let alone illnesses and accidents. It is a misleading comfort, if indeed it is a comfort at all, to say to bereaved children, 'God wanted her to come and live in heaven with Him.' How can they be expected to love a God who would be so selfish?

In awe and gratitude people sometimes find themselves able to say, 'This is the Lord's doing and it is marvellous in our eyes.'[21] If they really mean anything when they say this, they must have the courage to acknowledge a contrast and sometimes say in all reverence, 'This was not God's doing,' maybe even 'An enemy has done this.'[22]

Some horrors are bad enough without our having to try to persuade ourselves that God planned things so. W. H. Vanstone had a better teaching than that about the disaster at Aberfan:

> Our preaching on the Sunday after the tragedy was not of a God who, from the top of the mountain, caused or permitted, for his own inscrutable reasons, its disruption and descent; but of One Who received, at the foot of the mountain, its appalling impact, and Who, at the extremity of endeavour, will find yet new resources to restore and to redeem.[23]

7

The Creator who Takes Risks

He did not say: You will not be troubled, you will not be
belaboured, you will not be disquieted, but he said, You will
not be overcome.

Julian of Norwich, *Showings* 68

God *withdrawn?*

The day-to-day divine management of the universe need not after
all be a fundamental Christian doctrine. Christians are not
obliged to assume, against the evidence, that the Almighty is
concerned with pushing the furniture of the world about. It is a
relief not to have to think of oneself as Aladdin, with God as a sort
of genie of the magic lamp, so that there has to be some awkward
explaining when one's wishes are not granted.

It is all very well to quote Psalm 46, 'God is our hope and
strength: a very present help in trouble' for encouragement. We
dare not translate that assurance into an expectation that the
Lord will sort things out to our specifications. God's promised
presence is awesome, not obliging. When God speaks, human
concerns are superseded: 'the earth shall melt away.'[1]

Christian faith can afford to recognize that God does not
intervene in the ordinary workings of nature. God characteristically 'lets be'.[2] We know that God does not prevent people from
sinning. We ought to know that God does not prevent people
from being silly. It should not be a great jump to understand that
God does not prevent people from being unfortunate. The belief
that everything is 'meant', that nothing really happens by chance,
is superstitious, not religious. To say 'I've been lucky' is more
gracefully humble than to say 'God has looked after *me*,' which is
a bit too much like 'I bear a charméd life.'[3]

Religious people are apt to pick up inadequate notions of God just by trying to protect God from inadequate notions. They arrive at the idea that providence must be the real cause of everything that happens by thinking that it would be unworthy of God not to be in total control; so they fail to work out what they are really saying about God's purposes.

To some of our forebears, on the contrary, a remote God seemed a more reverent concept. They dared not imagine that the Almighty could be concerned with all the trivial matters which seem so important to human beings. The theory that God did make the world but takes no great interest in it was fashionable in the late seventeenth and eighteenth centuries under the name of *deism*.

With hindsight, historical deism looks like an unsatisfactory halfway house to modern atheism. It was a 'religion' without revelation, without miracles, without a saviour, more or less without grace. Why did high-minded intelligent people bother to affirm that they believed in God, when the Supreme Being they honoured had no role in their lives? Unless they were too timid or superstitious to be atheists, what was the point?

The point of deism was that atheism then hardly seemed a live option. Human beings wanted to know how this complex universe came into being: surely there had to be a Creator God to set things going? People who found the characteristic Christian doctrines incredible still felt obliged to hold on to this minimal belief. Before Darwin, the intricate well-adapted design of creatures seemed inexplicable without a designer. Unplanned eyes for seeing appeared as unlikely as a watch without a watchmaker. 'It is he that hath made us and not we ourselves.'[4]

Historically, what kept the deists believers was the argument from design, and Darwin put an end to this, opening the way to atheism. If eyes evolve because they are useful for survival, they do not need to be planned. Divine purpose becomes redundant. So the argument from design is now in shreds and that kind of deism has given way to a highly moral unbelief, which refuses to condone the amount of evil we find in creation. Instead of 'There must be a God to explain the world,' the urgent argument is now, 'How can there be a God who would allow all this misery?' The onus of proof has shifted. It is for believers to show that their creed is tenable. They can no longer ground their faith upon the evident ingenuity of the Creator.

Has deism lost all point now that atheism is easy for thinking people? Once nature seems self-explanatory, a remote First Cause no longer fills a theoretical need. The Supreme Being who takes no interest in the world can be phased out. But if the Christian God is not to be phased out too, the need to explain what kind of interest we believe God does take in the world is all the greater.

Christians affirm that 'God is Love' and the whole Bible is the story of what 'God is Love' means. There is work to be done to interpret that story and show how it can make sense of the world and is worth teaching to successive generations. The work is being impeded by a lush growth of implausible assumptions about every-day providences, and it is these which need to be cleared away.

When Christians claim special advantages in their daily lives it seems as if they are unwilling to inhabit the same bewildering and often unhappy world as their unbelieving contemporaries. When they witness to their faith they concentrate on what is least convincing. No wonder 'the heathen say: Where is now their God?'[5] Meanwhile the more promising message goes by default: the idea of a God who gives creatures space to be themselves, even to the point of taking risks that things may go wrong.

Of course this argument really is too difficult for children; but if only the adults could get it into their own heads that doubts about providence need not mean denying the gospel, they could be set free from the shaky and eventually defeatist pretence that because God loves people everything that happens to them must really be good for them. They would have a better chance of discovering the reality of God's help. We are rightly reluctant to unload grown-up troubles on to children or worry them with the cares of the world: but it is our duty to prepare them for living in the real world, troubles and all.

The God who lets be

Deism pictures God the Creator as founding and letting be. This would never do as the whole story, but it makes a good start. As Austin Farrer put it:

The universe is not a piece of streamlined engineering. It is meant to be what it is – a free-for-all of self-moving forces, each being itself with all its might.[6]

Suppose we allow, and indeed insist, that God did not plan the creation in every detail. Suppose we tell our children that God gave creatures room to be themselves.[7]

Scientists patronize believers nowadays for their presumed naivety. The story of creation in six days by the Word is assumed to be discredited science, contradicting the true story of evolution by chance through millions of years. Believers have invited this misunderstanding of their myth, by their slowness to catch inspiration from the vast scale of the creation as we now begin to picture it. They read the Book of Genesis expecting to find a God who made everything just so, rather than a God who 'makes the world make itself'.[8] They approve of the Big Bang as a way of starting a universe suddenly, but they do not approve of the random interplay of chance[9] as a way of letting creatures develop marvellous lives of their own. The world of Genesis may seem to us a smallish world, but it is more to the point that it was never a tame safe world.

Instead of a dogged faith which has to say that all sorts of bad things really show how good God is, a faith which is both more realistic and more exhilarating may be founded on the notion of a God who takes risks. Must that sound shocking? It can be expressed more biblically. 'We know that the whole creation has been groaning in travail together until now.'[10] In other words, God so loved the world that the risks of creating it were worthwhile. Making and venturing are ideas which fit well together.[11] God knows that things that are worth making can go wrong: and is willing to bear the cost.[12] To tell children that the world is God's great adventure makes better sense than to tell them that they had better not argue because God knows best.

The idea of God as Creator of creators is not shallow. This image can make some sense of the evils of the world; whereas the idea of God as the Great Planner who has everything arranged makes the organization of the world not exciting but merely inefficient. The question is not how creation can be safe, which it never was, but how creation can be worth the dangers and how the dangers are at last to be overcome.

This way of thinking sets us free to look at the creation afresh and see what it is really like, without having to say in advance what it must be like. The universe is strange and beautiful. To praise God for its glory begs fewer questions than to be grateful for favours received. Fortunate events might tempt me to presume that God made *me* a favourite; but the beauty of the world is for us all. To be grateful for it I do not have to indulge in vain imaginings. Thankfulness to whatever power is responsible is a good reaction, untainted by egotism.

We still have to take the rough with the smooth. We have no right to pick and choose as 'God-given' the bits we happen to like. Eventually we may hope that God can be approached in variegated ways, through the beauty and the terror of nature, and through the joys and the sorrows of ordinary life. But at present the route by way of everyday providence, which people expect to be so direct, is choked with hasty assumptions. The more roundabout route which starts from the notion of God the Creator is more promising.

If we think of the whole universe as God's creation, we can fit in gratefully whatever providences we may find: whereas if we begin with providence we cannot make sense of the whole universe. People whose central belief is that God takes care of human beings are bound to find the natural world a puzzling place. Why is nature so vast and so recalcitrant? What on earth is the point of it all? If on the contrary one begins with a larger idea of God as Maker of the universe, there is plenty of room in creation for every creature to be special, and for human beings to be, so to say, especially special.

God makes free creatures, who are real in their own right. Creation is not a sham, and there can be no guarantee that real creatures will behave according to God's will. God lets us choose: a platitude of which preachers are fond. If God is indeed the Maker of makers, the platitude comes to life. God's will does not simply unfold regardless of what human beings do. Instead of coming up against God's prefabricated purposes, people may discover that God's purposes are something they themselves are called upon to do something about. God's creatures may be honoured with the responsibility of being God's agents.

'But of course God arranges everything: God is omnipotent.' Anyone who clings to that version of God's glory soon finds all sorts of things going on which it seems impossible to believe that God could have planned. The small child is sure to start asking whether the Emperor has really done any arranging at all, and there is nothing to answer but 'Of course he has, although it doesn't look like it.'[13]

Why must people be so afraid to believe that God delegates? Timidity is no more reverent than boldness, and more dangerous, as it encourages the very scepticism it fears. The courage to say that God has courage affirms a more spacious creation: and indeed a creation more like the one we have got. The God who is incredible, not to be found either in our tradition or in our experience, is God the bureaucrat who regulates everything.

Real risks

It is still tempting to hanker after the idea that the risks are not quite real. People who tell the Christian story are so accustomed to the way it goes that they see it all as part of a great divine plan, never in doubt. Although creatures are free they will have to behave all right when it comes to the point. Of course the happy ending is on the way. Any little hitches are not very important. But when the little hitches are agonies and miseries, belittling them belittles God, and indeed slanders God, as if God were unconcerned.

An elementary way to take heed of the risks God runs in creation is to imagine Satan the adversary, pointing out that if something can go wrong, it will. Satan can always crab God's intentions for the world: 'You had better not. It's too dangerous. Just suppose . . . ' At every stage, God's plans are in peril. If people are not just puppets but real, suppose they are disobedient? Suppose God forgives sinful human beings and gives them a holy Law to live by, but they are stiff-necked? What happens if God's chosen representatives become possessive instead of generous? The corruption of the best is the worst, so it could turn out that the most faithful people will be the most set in their ways, unable to recognize the truth in front of their eyes. Suppose that when God's own Son comes to live among them, his welcome is short-lived? What if even his particular friends fail to understand? There could be a traitor among them. They might fail in a crisis and run away. Suppose the worst happens and he is killed? Suppose he does rise triumphantly from the tomb, but as the centuries go by the story repeats itself? The most righteous have the least imagination and show the least love. The earth is still 'full of darkness, and cruel habitations'.[14] All these fearful suppositions have come true: so the Christian story is not about plans put neatly into effect but about risks faced and overcome.

It is not true that if something can go wrong, it always will. Suppose God's messenger came to a young girl and told her that she was chosen to give birth to the Son of the Most High? Suppose she had responded 'No, no, this is too much for me,' and had turned away sorrowfully, like a certain promising young man?[15] Surely God would have found some other way, perhaps more painful. We do not know what God has done to make good the lost vocation of the rich young man. We do know that Christians have honoured Mary down the centuries as the Mother of the Lord. Gratitude need not ascribe a perfection to her which the New Testament does not, let alone divinity. Nor must it be compulsory to take literally the idea of the Angel Gabriel coming in visible tangible form to bring Mary God's message. Christians are not faithless if they take this as a legend, and tell it so to their children. What the story of the annunciation tells is that something could have gone wrong, and did not.

At each stage the risks God runs are real. The silly answer to Satan is to say, 'Oh, but there's no risk: it's all part of the plan.' A responsible Christian faith takes seriously the likelihood that the course of events is often contrary to God's will. When tiresome things happen, still more when dreadful things happen, trying to make out that God planned it all can only puzzle children and madden grown-ups. What Christians believe is that God knows the dangers even better than we do, and will always be one step ahead. The Christian hope is that the God who raised Jesus from the dead is able eventually to bring whatever happens to good.

Grace, providence and miracle

There are limits to God's 'letting be'. Christians believe that God did raise Jesus from the dead. Unless there is room in creation for God's mighty acts, Christian faith has been reduced beyond recognition. Thinking Christians too easily acquiesce in this reduction by assuming that if providence is difficult, miracles must be worse. Surprising as it may seem, it is quite consistent to cast doubt on providence and yet affirm that God can and does do miracles.

It is tidy but misleading to think of divine activity, as religious people hope to experience it, in a graded series from ordinary to extraordinary. The sequence would start with grace in what might be called its nuclear meaning, God's dealings with human beings. Next would come special providences, God's wonderful but not unusual control of external events. At the furthest from everyday experience, believers want to affirm miracles, God's extraordinary mighty works.[16]

When Christians take stock of their beliefs, they feel they ought to be confident about grace and providence; but they are allowed to find miracles more challenging. When they try to commend their beliefs to their secular contemporaries, grace and providence at least seem to make sense, but miracles are altogether too much. Believers would do well to rearrange the sequence and put the three kinds of divine activity in a different order of difficulty. If they accept that providence, the supposedly intermediate one, is the most doubtful of the three, they can set up grace and miracle on firmer foundations.

First of all, grace has to be firm. The conviction that God's grace is real, that there really is enough to go on, cannot be expendable for Christians. The availability of grace is already a large assertion. To take one's stand here is not a matter of making a modest claim, '"only" grace, no providence', and hoping to get away with it. Belief in God's grace strengthening us is more sustainable than belief in God's providence protecting us, not because grace does not mean very much, but because it accords better with the rest of what we believe. Grace becomes credible when it is fitted in to the whole picture of what faith in God means.

Miracles may become credible in a similar way. For most of us the reason for believing in God is the evidence of the religious tradition in which we stand. It is an integral part of that tradition, not an optional extra, that God has been revealed by mighty works. We are not asked to believe in just any mighty works, but in certain special interventions in the course of history: especially God's choosing and cherishing the Jewish people and the raising of Jesus from the dead. We do well to be sceptical about haphazard wonders scattered through the centuries, but when we hear tell of clusters of significant miracles we should at least attend to the evidence.

In the eyes of current secularism, the great error is to believe in God at all. If we are going to offend the spirit of the age we might as well, as Luther said, 'Pecca fortiter', 'sin strongly'.[17] Something 'supernatural' comes into our scheme of things with belief in God, if we can accept it. If we can take that first step, why rob it of significance by stopping there? How could we ever find out about a God who never did anything in particular? More robust conviction makes better sense, not worse.

What is wrong with the idea of providence is not that it is supernatural, but that people expect it to be ordinary. We have no reason to believe, and some reason not to believe, in an everyday force, short of miracle, into which our lives ought to be plugged. In other words, a 'special providence' is hardly a distinct idea from a miracle. It would be ungracious to deny that God sometimes grants people special favours which they rightly call 'providential'. What matters is that Christians ought not to expect such favours, and that Christians who never seem to experience anything like this are not second class.

It is natural to wish for miracles. Under stress we can hardly help praying for them. Sometimes miracles happen: but not predictably, still less controllably. Cautious agnosticism is better than jumping to conclusions and reticence is more becoming than hasty claims.

There is a world of difference between God tinkering with creation to get it properly adjusted, as if the world were an engine that constantly needed tuning, and God intervening wonderfully in creation to fulfil long-standing purposes. If people commending Christian belief kept this distinction clear in their own minds, faith would be less muddling for beginners.

8

Finding Grace

When God removes evils in the human sort of way, it is
commonly by the employment of human hands.

Austin Farrer[1]

God in charge

Is all this argument about a God who creates and lets be merely an
intellectual indulgence for argumentative modernists? On the
contrary, to set providence aside for practical purposes can be a
useful slimming exercise for sensible believers, who want the
ordinary diet they and their children feed on to be nourishing.

Grown-up and growing-up Christians need some idea of how
they believe God does act in the world, for the sake of their own
sincerity, let alone for convincing other people. To start with
doubts about providence does not mean to stop there. For a
recognizable Christian faith to be built on such a seemingly
unpromising foundation, a lot more needs to be said: in
particular, that God the Creator is still in charge. Christians who
refuse to say, 'Whatever has happened, God has done it,' should
go on to say instead: God takes responsibility for everything; God
enters into everything that happens; and above all, God is able in
the end to bring everything to good. These assertions are the
substance of the Christian faith. People who find them coherent
and credible have the duty to hand them down to those who come
after.

Suppose Christians start by putting aside the expectation of
everyday providences. They lay themselves open to the charge
that they have given way to deism, but they ought not to be
too worried. This kind of deism makes a good beginning. The
deist belief that the world has been made to run under its own

steam is realistic, as far as it goes, about what the creation is like.

Christians want to say a great deal more. They will have to leave deism behind: but not with precipitate haste. Its good start can be built on and its minimal theology can be enriched. The negative conviction that the Creator does not keep the world on a tight rein is a sensible way to begin.

The next step, the distinctively Christian step, is to add to the affirmation that God *makes* the world the conviction that God *enters into* the world and can be found there. God's patience need not mean God's absence.[2] There is nothing defeatist about the hope that our Creator will stand by us, not pushing us about but showing us things.[3]

The meaning of grace

Sitting loose to the idea of providence need not mean tumbling into scepticism. Grace is not lost. The primary meaning of grace, after all, is God's dealings with human beings. Christians who are doubtful about God's daily ordering of events can look expectantly for God's quiet inward influence on people. So far, so good. Believers can talk hopefully among themselves about grace; but unless they are happy to be members of an in-group they had better not take grace for granted as if its meaning were obvious. There is more exploring to be done.

A main problem about grace could be its apparent simplicity. A difficult word like 'redemption'[4] evidently has to be explained: but with grace we have the problem of not realizing that there *is* a problem. Religious people have a habit of wrapping up their faith in pious words like 'grace', which sound straightforward enough and are deemed to need no explaining. Sometimes the meaning is so well wrapped that it does not often get taken out and inspected. It may seem better to be vague about God's grace, because anything too definite would be unworthy of God. That is how the word 'grace' is dispensed from the duty to bring a distinct picture to mind.

We are all supposed to know more or less what grace is. Its most ordinary meaning is graceful movement, like ballet, which is plain enough but unhelpful for characterizing the grace of God.

'Grace' is used metaphorically, but still means human graceful-
ness, when we say 'She did it all with a good grace.' 'You might
have the grace to say you are sorry' may begin to have something
to do with heavenly help. When grace is linked with favour, it
looks still more like something which comes down from on high.
A 'grace and favour house' belongs to the Queen and a subject is
allowed to live in it. Royal graces and favours are supposed to be
modelled on divine graces and favours: but God's grace is less
solid than a house.

Is God's grace just God's favour? Does God have favourites as
kings notoriously do? People say things like, 'There but for the
grace of God go I.' They say this humbly, meaning 'Without
God's grace I should be stuck in my bad old ways. I could not
have been what I am now.' But sometimes people appropriate
God's grace too easily, looking at other people who are plainly in
a bad way and presumably are short of grace. The suggestion that
'God decided to back up one faulty human being, me, with special
protection, while letting that other poor sinner cope unaided'
casts a lot of doubt upon the fairness of God. It matters that
Christians should think what they say, because they already have
a reputation for being smug and naive.

Amazing grace

Some Christians would find this enquiry about the meaning of
grace extraordinary. The undeserved and wonderful grace of
God through Jesus Christ is what the Christian faith means to
them. They know themselves to be sinners and they have
discovered that their Redeemer has come to their rescue. The
story Bunyan told in *The Pilgrim's Progress*, of how the burden of
sins fell off at the foot of the cross, answers to their experience.
There is a great Christian tradition, all the way back to St Paul, of
believers whose faith began with repentance in the strong sense of
turning in a new direction, who have spent the rest of their days
glorifying God in gratitude. This experience of grace is neither
unreal nor outdated: for those who have actually had it. It is not
the only meaning of grace nor the only valid way to find grace;
and for children it is most unlikely to be the best way in to faith.

The best way to set off for any destination depends upon where one is. We hope that children will not be starting out on their pilgrimage with a huge consciousness of sin. For grown-up people with a lack of interest in anything spiritual, or with intellectual difficulties about whether 'spiritual' has any meaning, or both, it is unrealistic to expect them to begin with gratitude that their sins are forgiven. They are sincerely conscious that they are leading quite virtuous lives, and they are not feeling oppressed by the burden of sinfulness. It is scarcely ethical to set about giving people a sense of sin just in order to take it away again. When impressionable people are under one's authority or influence, it may even be manipulative to preach to them this version of the Good News.

The Christian faith is comprehensive enough to be able to answer many different questions. If people are not asking, 'How can I get rid of my sins?' but 'Where is God anyway? Does God do anything? What *is* "grace"?' it may be positively unwholesome to try to convict them of wickedness rather than attempt to give them a rational answer. If they could begin to grasp the generosity of God, then they could begin to see the meaning of sin.

Of course sin is not to be belittled. 'All we like sheep have gone astray.'[5] It is impossible to start to understand the meaning of God's grace without becoming aware, by contrast, of one's own unworthiness. For many of us today that is the right way round. Minds and hearts do not have to be at odds. If first we show one another things,[6] repentance can turn out to be, not an embarrassing hurdle but a natural response.

Means of grace

English Christians down the centuries who have used the General Thanksgiving[7] have been accustomed to thank God for providing '*means* of grace'. They express their gratitude, not for God's individual favours but for God's availability. They give thanks to God for being findable: in other words, for giving us ways of getting in touch.

In the Prayer Book context, the Christian sacraments are the God-given 'means of grace'. Faithful Christians ought to avoid a tempting short cut here, or they may make it appear to everyone else that God's availability has shrunk into something churchy. It is a pity to be so grateful for the sacraments that the idea of 'means of grace' disappears into technicality. The way to get in touch with God, instructed Christians naturally want to explain, is to use the means God has provided, the church service called the eucharist, the holy communion or the mass. Communicant Christians may be happy to settle down here straight away, but they will be no help to anyone else if they take refuge too quickly in what looks like ritualism. They will never succeed in rescuing 'grace' from its everyday vagueness by embarking forthwith upon specialized talk about what happens in church.

The technical language of eucharistic theology is a big jump from the comfortable language of piety. Into that gap comprehension falls and gets lost. Since 'theology' is anyway expected to be impossibly obscure, it seems less trouble just to be vague about the grace of God, to let it mean something but never mind what, rather than try to discover what it is and where it can be found.

Once people are seriously asking, 'How can human beings hope to get in touch with God?' the ancient 'means of grace', the sacraments, may indeed become a main part of the answer.[8] The sacraments could never be the whole answer, because they presuppose a good deal of understanding. Ceremonies, however time-honoured, cannot stand up on their own. It would be pointless to say that grace is conveyed by particular rites, unless we first had a reasonably distinct idea of God-given grace as something possible to impart.

Alert Christians ought to pounce on this way of putting it: 'some*thing* possible to impart'. Is this the real reason why grace seems difficult to comprehend? No wonder our faith seems unreal and mechanical, if we imagine grace as a *thing*. It is hopeless to think of God's grace as something distinct from God.[9] If the notion of 'means of grace' had to lead straight to a picture of grace as some sort of material stuff, then it would be time to find some different terminology.

All human terminology over-simplifies. The most promising over-simplification is to say that God's grace *is* God: God as findable. Since God is not an object just sitting there for us to investigate, getting in touch with God must need God's co-operation, and God's co-operation is what we really mean by the grace of God. God's help is necessary for finding God, and 'means of grace' are, as it were, the arrangements God makes for providing help.

There is no need to think of grace as a shapeless substance like lava flowing out of a volcano; nor like the water supply laid on by the church, available on tap, with or without 'the noise of the water-pipes'.[10] Nor is grace a sort of gift-wrapped parcel God has ready to hand over to us if we ask nicely. Increasing understanding needs a combination of care and boldness. The care means not hastily writing off the whole matter, even if we have to be patient in unravelling well-meaning confusion. The boldness means not shying timidly away from possible illumination. The question of grace is the question of what practical difference faith in God is supposed to make.

Unobtrusive reality

Once grace is distinguished from providence, the idea of God as a power pulling the strings of a great puppet-show can lose its grip. People can be set free to look for a different sort of God who may be found upholding them whatever does happen. As long as they think God does everything, they must imagine God as, so to say, up against them. When the Almighty will not grant their wishes, they just have to adjust their wishes to what God does give them, but it is hard to be truly thankful. A God who does not organize all the changes and chances of life from behind the scenes is nearer and more accessible as 'a very present help in trouble',[11] and not only in trouble but in happiness, in perplexities and struggles, fears and aspirations, disappointments and successes.

God's providential ordering of events is almost an extra in comparison. Believers hope that God will somehow get in touch with them. Of course they hope that things will go well for them; but still more, whether outward things go well or badly, they want God to whisper in their ears.

But does God whisper in our ears? Is it really more realistic to hope for God's presence and guidance than to hope for special providences? Has the Emperor any clothes on?[12] It can be unnecessarily hard to get at the truth about whether grace really is available, because those who could best answer this question are apt to be reluctant to attend to it. People who want to be faithful refuse to admit that there could be a problem: 'Of course we experience God's grace'; upon which people who most want to emphasize honesty play Cordelia[13] and stand, maybe negatively, on their integrity: 'We won't say anything more than we must.'

It is fatally easy to set faith and honesty in opposition to each other. It is especially easy when it is especially dangerous, when we want to smooth the way for the little ones and not say anything to upset them. Rather than batter them with arguments, let alone with technical terms like 'deism', it seems simpler to tell children about a God who talks to us like an ordinary human being, and let them do the worrying when the facts fail to fit.

People who would not dream of leaving sharp knives lying around in case exploring children should cut themselves are quite capable of leaving frightening logical questions lying around. Am I too hopeless to hear what God is saying to me? – or do grown-up people not care about the truth? The sensible policy is not to banish either knives or arguments out of the kingdom like spindles, in the vain hope of evading the bad fairy's curse, but to provide contexts for learning their responsible use.

If faith and honesty are willing to co-operate instead of taking up contrary positions, they ought to be perfectly capable of talking the same language, and saying quite simple things in it. There are good reasons why God's grace is likely to be quiet and unobtrusive, harder to identify than believers might hope. What sort of world would it be, in which God spoke loud and clearly?

Human beings are obliged to make efforts to be open with one another, because human communication is always imperfect, restricted by human limitations. We cannot be everywhere; we cannot tell people what we do not know; we cannot always hear or be heard, even by telephone; we constantly exercise choices about whether, when and how to get in touch. However 'outgoing' we want to be, availability for some people necessarily makes us less available for others. But God's 'outgoingness' is not restricted by limitations: only by God's own choice. Once we think on these lines, it becomes inconceivable that God would take over all situations, intervene in every conversation, tell us everything, never let up, shout us all down . . . To give creatures any life of their own, God has to exercise self-restraint.

Is it therefore so hard to believe that God does exercise self-restraint, to the extent of being quite elusive? 'Verily thou art a God that hidest thyself.'[14] If we want to encourage one another, we ought to be more careful not to build up misleading expectations. The picture of a Christian as a secretary taking dictation is hopeless. Whether for grown-ups or children, the picture of a bird-watcher sitting quiet and still to see what will appear is far more promising.

9

Enough to Go On

Christ doth call
One and all:
Ye who follow shall not fall.

Robert Bridges

Glimpses

Just as we do not need clinching proof but enough to go on,[1] so
we do not need high-powered 'religious experience' but enough
for making a start. The questions are, how much *is* enough, and
do we have that much? This is where faith must make a serious
effort to be more honest than faith sometimes is about where we
really stand. It is fair to say that for most of us belief is grounded
mainly upon trusting other people. We trust the testimony of
prophets and saints which has been handed on to us, and we trust
those contemporary believers who are wiser and more perceptive
than we are.

For other people's experience to be enough to go on, it needs to
be grounded, sooner or later, in something real of one's very own.
Without being egotistically autobiographical, a Christian has an
obligation not to sheer off the question, 'What is it like for you?' If
other Christians, children and grown-ups, are too shy or polite to
ask, sooner or later they need to know what ground there is in
ordinary experience for the faith believers profess.

Shallow over-confidence makes communication unnecessarily
difficult, whether among contemporaries or between generations. 'Of course God talks to us, if only we listen': and fellow
Christians, young and old, who have no such confidence can only
be silent and feel inadequate. George Herbert's faith is more
encouraging, because when he could not find God he said so:

75

O that thou shouldst give dust a tongue
To cry to thee,
And then not hear it crying! All day long
My heart was in my knee,
But no hearing.[2]

So he can be trusted when he tells what he has found.

Integrity is not obliged to be negative. There is a kind of receptiveness which is just as sincere, which looks to see what is there: which is willing to be encouraged. A Christian life can be built up, bit by bit, out of small hints and glimpses on a foundation of tradition.[3] The depths and heights are evident enough, when people find themselves falling or soaring, but a great deal of human life is somewhere in between. It matters whether God can be found in ordinariness.

Face to face encounters with the Almighty are not ordinary. Accept that fact, and there is more chance of finding a more unobtrusive God who is somewhere nearby, perhaps at one's elbow or looking over one's shoulder, clearing away nonsense, puncturing pomposity, suddenly claiming an easily-given pledge, sharing a little joke, pointing something out, or just saying 'Hush'. There are moments when one has an idea, not merely second-hand, of what worship might be. The smallness of these glimpses, their triviality, even their unworthiness of God's greatness, are what make them convincing. If God does get in touch with human beings in an everyday way God has to become very small in order not to overwhelm us.

There is nothing so grand here as an 'argument from religious experience'. There is nothing to presume upon, no proof here for anyone else, but a modest rebuttal, for one's own need, of the atheist argument that a lack of religious experience *dis*proves God. A tiny positive awareness, vouchsafed gradually over the years, can count against the sceptical accusation, 'You have no idea what you are talking about.'[4] This small-scale account of where many of us stand fits well with St Paul's 'now we see through a glass, darkly; but then face to face.'[5]

To begin like this ought to be less daunting for young Christians than more ambitious specifications of 'the spiritual life'. C. S. Lewis and Austin Farrer have both left accounts of the desperation they experienced in youth when they had erroneous expectations of what prayer ought to be. C. S. Lewis battled in vain for 'realizations'; and for years took refuge thankfully in atheism.[6] Austin Farrer's religious upbringing led him to expect some kind of face-to-face colloquy with God. What set him free was reading Spinoza.[7] When he failed to hear God's voice addressing him through Bible reading or prayer, Spinoza's notorious 'pantheism', God in all, gave him the hint he needed.

Austin Farrer did not begin to have conversations with God, but he did arrive at belief in God as the underlying cause of his thinking and especially of his attempts to think about God. The frustration of dutifully trying to meet God face to face was cured by the hope that sometimes his own thoughts

> would become diaphanous . . . as a deep pool, settling into a
> clear tranquillity, permits us to see the spring in the bottom of it
> from which its waters rise.[8]

Is it too difficult to try to explain to children that God will show them things through the depths of their own thinking? Superficially it is simpler to tell them to talk to Jesus: too simple, because it gives them the notion of a God who is just like another human being, but who oddly enough never talks back: a bothersome notion which puts down deep roots and is hard to eradicate.

There is no reason for surprise that we have no proof of God's presence, only clues. God's grace does not depend upon people noticing it.[9] If it is true that God is more likely to enlighten and strengthen us from within than to meet us face to face, we may truly be enlightened and strengthened, without always knowing that we are. In time, or maybe in eternity, we can look back and recognize the help we had.

The pure in heart are promised that one day they shall see God.[10] Meanwhile there is encouragement in the story of Moses who asked to see God's glory, and was allowed to wait in a crevice of the rock and see God's back.[11] St Gregory of Nyssa applied this to Christian disciples: 'He who follows will not turn aside from the right way if he always keeps the back of his leader in view.'[12] Following is surely an easier image to apply than meeting. Anyone who has seen which way the leader went can try to follow, without fretting about where and when one is going to arrive, or whether other people are pursuing different routes. 'What is that to thee? Follow thou me!'[13]

Finding God in conscience?

Following in the right way is a congenial idea for English Christians. We feel we know where we are with it. It suggests everyday ideas about 'being good' rather than exotic notions of 'religious experience'. It begins to look as if following Christ really means much the same as following conscience, and so we can talk about our belief in a style which feels natural: so natural that we ought to be a little careful not to make conscience too godlike.

Morality is central in our faith, so no wonder we expect God's communication with us to take the form of moral enlightenment. But morality is something we are apt to think we understand already, so no wonder it becomes tempting to tell one another that finding God is quite easy after all. All the careful talk about finding God in hints and glimpses can seem unnecessarily timid to people who are moralists at heart. Why not affirm boldly that we can all get to know God by listening to God's voice speaking to us in our consciences?

The most obvious snag about this is the human tendency to put words into God's mouth. Christians who know about right and wrong are confident about what conscience will say without having to pay careful attention. So faithful believers are tempted to complacency: any new message will be for other people.

Of course this is a caricature and faithful believers try to be humble, not arrogant. The trap they are as likely to fall into is boredom: God speaks plainly enough but never says anything fresh or surprising. The words they put into God's mouth are a suitable selection of their own words.

People quite expect conscience to speak in platitudes, and what happens next is that some faithful people become anxious when the platitudes seem too easy. They dare not let their consciences utter agreeable platitudes that they would like to hear. They know that smooth words are dangerous: so they jump to the conclusion that God's voice speaking through conscience is bound to say something unwelcome, never encouraging. That is how moralism sneaks in and gains a firm foothold. Living a good life is reduced to the negative aim of keeping this reproachful voice within us quiet.

Children readily grasp the notion that God tells them about right and wrong: sometimes they grasp it too readily. It is easy to convey to a child ideas about conscience and God which coalesce into a tyranny. A child was reproached by her mother for a small social gaffe, and felt haunted by mortification. When she said to another grown-up, 'Don't we sometimes feel awful about something we've done?' the answer was 'Yes, that's conscience'; upon which she felt worse than ever. That was an unlucky misunderstanding, but not surprising when what conscience means for many people is indeed 'feeling awful'. If conscience is the voice of God, God is someone who makes one feel horribly embarrassed. Our human parents are on our side and proud of us, but not our heavenly Father. Piety and shame are intertwined, required and taboo both at once. It is no wonder if people who are growing up and starting to think for themselves are not particularly enthusiastic about the idea of hearing God's voice.

More destructively, one way to keep conscience quiet is to try, consciously or not, to shift the 'feeling awful' on to somebody else. Blaming one another comes naturally to human beings.[14] When the threatening burden of guilt has to be shifted somehow, the simplest answer is to

> compound for sins they are inclin'd to
> By damning those they have no mind to.[15]

People with selective consciences appear hypocritical and censorious. The reason why they seem to pick on other people's sins may be that they are fighting a somewhat desperate rearguard action against self-condemnation. They become a menace when they ascribe divine authority to their own censored way of looking at the world. Their conscientiousness poses the harsh question, Does God never speak to those others who see things differently, or are the others ignoring the voice within?

Meanwhile sceptics make out a plausible case that God's voice is imaginary and that the 'conscience' which gives people such an uncomfortable time is an arbitrary left-over from their upbringing. Certainly anyone who considers the terrible things some people have done when they have obeyed this voice within them will be wary of giving conscience too high a status.

All this anxiety is unnecessary if people stop trying to believe or to get their children to believe that conscience is God's voice. My conscience is my own self, concentrated into a moral whole.[16] Unbelievers and believers alike can think of conscience on these lines and go on variously to qualify and explain. Children can begin to understand the meaning of integrity. Philosophers can discuss what one's 'own self' is and what 'moral' means. Freudians can inform us about how conscience is formed, and make sure that we remember the power of unconscious desires and the likelihood of self-deception. Theologians can allow themselves to learn from all these insights.

What Christians need to grasp is not that conscience is God's infallible voice, but that 'conscience' is a way of talking about the God-given human capacity to want to be good and to try to be good. As Bishop Butler put it, we have 'the rule of right within'.[17]

Conscience is one's own voice, not directly God's. What it tells people can partly depend on all sorts of chances of their upbringing and experience. Conscience can be deceived and even distorted, and its authority can be abused. What conscience means at its best is the developed moral integrity of a human being. To be governed by conscience is to put one's heart into living by the best light one has seen so far.

What becomes then of people's search for God's guidance? Attending to conscience is an important kind of attention. We can hope to hear God's voice in conscience without supposing that conscience *is* God. God can be present to human beings in their moral understanding, simple or deep, in the same kind of way as God can enter into their joys and sorrows, thoughts and wishes, their experience of beauty or their concern for other people.

For most of us, God is more likely to whisper than to shout. We have no hot line. We must not try to use our conscientious certainties as proof that God really is talking to us. On the other hand, people who are convinced that God does talk to them cannot use that conviction as proof that what they hear their consciences telling them to do is bound to be right.

Sometimes when we do not know what to do we may hope that God will use our consciences to enlighten us. Sometimes we may approach from the opposite direction and believe that our innate awareness of right and wrong is a clue to the reality of God; but we cannot conflate these moves and try to go both ways at once. What believers can encourage one another to hope is that if they attend carefully God will inspire them with good ideas which will sometimes be different from what they have been saying to themselves so far.

Giving thanks always for all things[18]

Surely it is still more important for Christians to be grateful and encourage one another to be grateful? Doubts about providence, and reduced expectations of everyday encounters with God, might suggest thin gratitude. On the contrary, it is worth reiterating that if Christians are grateful for what they have found, not for what they think they should expect to find, their gratitude has meaning.[19] All-purpose thankfulness is self-defeating.

The atheist philosopher Antony Flew was rightly severe[20] about what a bad example religious people set by irresponsibly disregarding facts. They talk about God's loving care; something dreadful happens; so they just change the meaning of 'loving care'. Whatever the world is like, nothing is allowed to count against God's love. So 'God's love' ceases to mean anything in particular, and faith dies the 'death by a thousand qualifications'.[21] This kind of criticism ought to make Christians careful not to go about saying that everything that happens shows how much God loves them. It is sensible not to claim too much: but if that were the whole story it would be unduly defeatist.

It must be better to be grateful than ungrateful. Believers and unbelievers alike will be the poorer, if in the name of logical caution we high-mindedly discourage people from expressing appreciation for their blessings. There is a kind of grateful frame of mind which looks around for someone to thank.

Robert Louis Stevenson gave a delightful illustration. Travelling in the Cevennes, he had camped happily among pine trees under the stars, and wanted to express his gratitude:

> I hastened to prepare my pack, and tackle the steep ascent that lay before me; but I had something on my mind. It was only a fancy; yet a fancy will sometimes be importunate. I had been most hospitably received and punctually served in my green caravanserai. The room was airy, the water excellent, and the dawn had called me to a moment. I say nothing of the tapestries or the inimitable ceiling, nor yet of the view which I commanded from the window; but I felt I was in some one's debt for all this liberal entertainment. And so it pleased me, in a laughing way, to leave pieces of money on the turf as I went along, until I had left enough for my night's lodging. I trust they did not fall to some rich and churlish drover.[22]

This kind of gratitude cannot be made to bear any logical weight, as if the existence of God could be proved from our feeling grateful. Nor is human thankfulness to be colonized, as if it meant that we are all believers at heart. Yet surely Christians may hope that the God whom they worship will accept this appreciative attitude to life as one valid kind of praise.

Another sort of thankfulness is the instinct to say 'non nobis': 'Not unto us, O Lord, not unto us, but unto thy Name give the praise'.[23] When people have been taught that all good is God's doing, not theirs, it would be mean-spirited to discourage them from saying thank-you to God. After the Battle of Agincourt in Shakespeare's *Henry V*, the King calls for the list of the English dead and exclaims in awestruck humble relief, 'O God! thy arm was here.'[24] How seemly after a great victory to sing Non nobis and Te Deum. It would be a shame to spoil the story by treating such faith as a mistake. It is also seemly to stand back eventually and wonder what to say to a bereaved French mother that day: surely not 'Our God gave us the victory to punish your leaders for gloating.'

A proper gratitude ought to be more ready to find God's grace than to claim God's grace. 'God is here, blessing me in this way': not 'God decided to bless me rather than the others.' Finding God in victory is dangerously easy, though not therefore wrong. Finding God in defeat is harder, though not impossible.

No human situation is complete in itself. There is always more to come which may ruin or redeem what has happened up to now. To be able at last to look back and see how a disaster has been made good may be as great a blessing as to celebrate a triumph. When what is going on now seems impenetrably meaningless, Christians should not say hastily, 'There is no God' or 'God has gone away,' or worse still, 'This is what God wanted.' More hopefully they can say, 'God knows all about it. God will help. God can make something even out of this mess.'

Presence rather than purpose

There is no need, however, for believers to defer all their hopes to the far future, one day, when God will make all things well. Instead they may adopt an encouraging slogan: *Look for presence rather than purpose.* 'God is with us': not 'God arranged it.' If it turns out that they can discern purpose too, so well and good; but there is no need to hunt, anxiously or obstinately, for short-run divine meaning in evidently untoward happenings.

A little sermon about sparrows may clarify the distinction between purpose and presence. Faithful Christians have been glad to believe that our God knows what happens to every sparrow[25] and therefore, how much more, knows what happens to us who are God's children. In the King James Bible and the Revised Version Jesus says, 'Not one of them will fall to the ground without your Father.' Whatever happens, God is there. The new translations[26] fill in 'your Father's will' or 'your Father's leave', tipping the balance, less encouragingly, from God's presence to God's purpose, making us wonder why God wants the sparrows to be shot down.

We might tip the balance gently back towards presence again, not by haggling over more or less literal translations of the Greek, but by thinking of what John Keats said about another sparrow: 'I take part in its existence and peck about the Gravel.'[27] If a human poet's creative imagination could enter into the sparrow's experience, how much more, we may well say, can our Creator enter into our experience and take part in our existence, since we are of more value than many sparrows.

There is a positive side to denying that all events are God's doing. The question 'Where is God?' can sometimes be answered, not 'Everywhere', which may not mean much, but 'Here'. Not having to be thankful for absolutely everything allows people to be thankful in particular. The Chief Rabbi Jonathan Sacks, in an article in *The Times*, quoted an ancient saying that God is not everywhere but 'where we let Him in'.[28]

Rudolf Otto in *The Idea of the Holy* was wisely critical of the notion that God has to be everywhere. We do not get that idea from the Bible. The God who is to be found in the Bible is 'the God who is where he wills to be, and is not where he wills not to be,' the God who 'comes and goes, approaches and withdraws' and is sometimes far away and sometimes near.[29] God is not glorified by a blanket insistence that all places and situations are much of a muchness to God. Finding God's presence ought to need discernment.

Many Christians have gratefully learnt to find God in what has been called 'the sacrament of the present moment'.[30] Some take this to mean that whatever happens to them must be God's gift. It is just as good or better if it means that whatever happens, God can come to meet them. Some people seem to have learnt how to consecrate every circumstance of their lives, like the bread and wine of holy communion, as a means of grace. For them, there is nowhere too unpropitious for God's presence: not 'God arranges', but 'God accepts invitations'.

That is a bare statement, not even easy to understand, still less obvious. If it is to become part of the faith we are able to hand on, it needs filling in and backing up. Belief in the sustaining presence of God cannot be self-sustaining. 'How do you know?' is a fair question. If people are too docile to ask it while they are young, by the time they have gained the necessary confidence they may have drawn their own negative conclusions.

Some people do not need to search for God because they have the experience of being found, not always willingly. They say things like 'Whither shall I go then from thy Spirit?'[31] or 'I fled Him down the nights and down the days.'[32] For some people the creation is transparent and everything in it speaks of God. Their conviction, strenuous or easy, is so powerful that it can be an encouragement to people who are searching that there is indeed something to be found; but not, surely, an excuse to let people off from doing any searching of their own at all.

For most of us, the foundation of faith must be the evidence of many people's experience,[33] backed up by whatever hints we have found for ourselves.[34] There are plenty of witnesses to be called: prophets, mystics, poets, saints, who have been conscious of God's presence. Perhaps these may give us enough to go on: perhaps not. Christians have something particular to add. For Christians, God was present most plainly in the life, death and resurrection of Jesus Christ. When they are challenged to show reason for the hope that is in them,[35] that is where their answer will be concentrated.

10

Finding God in Christ

If I could find that god, he would hear and answer.

Edwin Muir[1]

Christ is born in Bethlehem

It is high time for the keystone to be lowered into place. The building so far would hardly stand up without it. The bare statement that God the Creator is responsible for everything[2] will hardly convince anyone who is not already well on the way to conviction. Affirmations about a God of love are no use without some indication of what on earth this means.

To counter the negative argument that if God were real God would do something, Christians are apt to feel that they ought to talk about special providences or strong 'religious experiences'. What they should say is that God did do something: God acted in Jesus Christ.

Christians tell the story of the life, death and resurrection of Jesus, and so they can be realistic about the way the world generally goes. Their faith need not be undermined when they notice that every particular blessing for one human being seems to be balanced by ghastly nightmares for other no less deserving human beings. It is true, though not the whole truth, to say that the Creator does not generally intervene.

If we have come to think that daily providential interventions are the wrong sort of activity for God, we should not therefore suppose that God does not act: it is even more important to think about how God does act. When believers feel obliged to deny some traditional ideas, they ought to be all the more careful to make plain what they positively affirm. They ought never to give the impression that doubt is a package deal. It is no wonder that the honourable stance called 'liberalism' has come to have a bad name, when people who admit to any uncertainties go on to do a sort of demolition job, as if they were saying, 'as well be hanged for a sheep as a lamb'.

The point of the belief that Jesus Christ was and is both divine and human is that God the Creator is not an absentee landlord. God does not just sit on high watching the course of events, but comes into the course of events as a human being. People who affirm the 'two natures' of Christ are not being obstinate or feebly conformist. The doctrine did become difficult and technical with human attempts to pin it down and exclude errors;[3] but it need not be essentially abstruse. Many indeed find it naive. It comes into its own as a promising answer to questions like: Where can we find God? How do we know that God takes any interest in the world after setting it going?

If people are not worried by this kind of question about how to find God, then the concept of finding God in Christ may not, for them, be an answer. They ought not to be blamed or patronized. Believers who belong to other traditions, and some Christians who sit loose to orthodoxy, can bow down before God's greatness and discover God's compassion in different ways. If God was truly in Christ, then God is available in Christ, but heaven forbid that Christians should suppose that God is available only in Christ. What is available does not have to be compulsory. The more wonderful its availability, the less need to think of it as compulsory. St Paul's 'he emptied himself'[4] is inspiration, not ammunition for a heresy hunt.

'Uniqueness' is a concept to handle carefully. Christians affirm that of all human beings, Jesus alone is God the Son. If that is true, it is true for everyone; but can Christians dare to admit that it might not be equally relevant for everyone? The incarnation is assuredly not the whole truth about God: might other truths about God answer better to what some people need? Some of us hope that it may also be true that Mohammed is God's prophet. If so, since Mohammed did not claim to be God's only prophet, the 'people of the Book' could honour one another more than their stormy histories might suggest.

People who deny what is actually true, or affirm what is not true, are actually mistaken, even if they never discover this. Intolerance begins, not with affirming one's beliefs, nor even with thinking that other people are mistaken, but with supposing that one has the whole truth, thinking in slogans, assuming incompatibility, refusing to look for convergence, taking credit and ascribing blame.

Critical Christians are reluctant to affirm that the doctrine of the 'two natures' is true. They are out of sympathy with it, ecumenically or metaphysically or both, and would like to manage without it. Meanwhile the simple kind of Christianity which is dismissively called 'folk religion' is not so defeatist. While theologians grumble, children enact the paradox of God made man every Christmas. A doll in a child's arms represents 'the Maker of the stars and sea',[5] 'the Word within a word, unable to speak a word',[6] who enters human understanding as 'Baby Jesus'.

God does not just take human *form* and act the part of a man, knowing all the time that this is only a performance. God takes human *flesh*. 'Enfleshing' is what 'incarnation' means. Far from being an abstract notion at home in a dead language, it is, precisely, down to earth. God living a real human life with difficulties and hurts is a good deal easier to explain to children than the idea of a bodiless God whom we can never see or hear, who never apparently does anything, but who has to be praised all the same.

To be fair, it is not mere defeatism which makes thinking Christians anxious about the traditional faith that Jesus is God incarnate. How could the human life of God not be a sham? Pious ways of talking about Jesus have given the impression that he must have been play-acting all the while. Not surprisingly, many people believe that it is more reverent after all to emphasize his complete humanity, and then say in the end that he had some sort of special relationship with God. They do not want to risk making him inhuman by insisting that he was actually God in person.

Austin Farrer made a suggestion[7] about this difficulty. There is a philosophical distinction between 'knowing that' and 'knowing how'. The teacher knows *that* 'la maison' is the French for 'the house', and can tell the children so. She also knows *how* to speak French, but this kind of knowledge is not so simple to communicate to the children. Knowing how to ride a bicycle is just as real as knowing that this bicycle is yours; but unless I try I am not sure whether I still know how, and even if I do, I cannot put it into words. Farrer suggested that the knowledge which Jesus, who was God-made-man, needed was *how* to be God. Christians may believe that Jesus was both truly human and truly divine, without having to suppose that he had, at every moment, an experience of being divine.

In the story of the temptation in the wilderness, the devil says, '*If* you are the Son of God, command these stones to become loaves of bread.'[8] The sting is in the 'if'. If Jesus were *not* really the Son of God, or if all the while he knew clearly *that* he was the Son of God, the temptation would be pointless. There is no need to imagine a traditional devil with horns and a tail to believe that Jesus Christ was beset by real, and probably recurrent,[9] temptation to put his status to the test.

Of course these notions are naive: how could they not be? They make sense for people who are prepared to take seriously the idea that God might live a human life. That idea emerges out of the New Testament as the best way of doing justice to the experience of the first followers of Christ, the people on the spot. Their theology is not monochrome: its diversity has been much emphasized lately;[10] but what they offer is a composite picture of a man who was more than a man, in whom human beings can find God.

Light and life to all he brings

'Folk religion' is happy with the baby in the manger who brings to earth the grace of God. The story of the nativity is about the two natures of Christ, whether or not it is garnished with ox and ass, shepherds and eastern sages, northern holly and ivy, even snow and sleigh-bells. In the context of Christmas, the idea that Jesus is both divine and human is not abstract, academic, and abstruse, but down to earth, practical and eminently suitable for children.

People who want to teach Christianity as a simple faith are not so happy when Jesus grows up. What did the Son of God come into the world to do? If we say that he came to die, what was the point of that? Is there any good news in the gospel for twentieth-century children, if good works are dreary, suffering is gloomy, sin is unhealthy, death is alarming, and miracles are incredible?

A doctrine of incarnation, God made flesh, is incomplete without a doctrine of atonement, God reconciling. When Christians were struggling to define the meaning of the two natures of Christ and the Three-in-Oneness of God, they never produced an official definition of the meaning of atonement. For this we may be thankful, since their theological struggles were so apt to take ferocious political shape.

There are therefore various optional ways of understanding the meaning of the death of Christ. Was it a sacrifice, a rescue, a victory over the devil, the settling of a debt, a punishment accepted on behalf of sinners, an illustration of what love means, or what? Surely the cross may have many meanings, and new generations of believers can surely find new ways of looking at it, to see how this dreadful death could somehow do something about what is wrong with the world.

All the theories of atonement are conditioned by the frames of mind of the human beings who thought them up, but are none the worse for that if we are willing to try to think historically. Even the idea which to our way of thinking is particularly unpromising, that the cross was a 'satisfaction' for sin,[11] makes more sense, and becomes more accessible, when it is connected with ideas of honour in a feudal society. We rightly find it incredible that the Son of God died to propitiate his angry Father. We have to repudiate the unworthy idea of an irascible God who demands 'satisfaction'; but must we lose touch with the idea of God's honour, what we might nowadays call God's integrity? Sin is a blot on God's beloved creation. The Holy One is not merely offended but dishonoured by human badness: therefore God's merciful forgiveness must have a more serious meaning than 'Never mind'. Human beings set about explaining that seriousness in terms of kinds of relationship which are already familiar to them.

11

God With Us

Surely he hath borne our grief, and carried our sorrows.

Isa. 53.4

God and sinners reconciled

People who are not haunted by their sins, who are not longing to be reconciled with God, are likewise not longing to understand the meaning of atonement. They may prefer to think as little as possible about the way Jesus died, and certainly not worry or frighten children about it. Crucifixion was part of the cruel behaviour of people long ago. Christians can think of Good Friday as a dreadful warning of what the violence in human nature can do: but do we have to believe that the cross has actually made a difference? Must we perplex ourselves with trying to elucidate what difference it has made?

The easiest way for twentieth-century Christians to start thinking about the death of Christ is to look on it as an example: a clear picture of what God's love is like. Do beginners need to go on from that to engage themselves with theories of atonement? We are told to 'meet people where they are'. Since not many of our contemporaries are enquiring about how to get rid of their sins, do we have to make the cross so central in our faith any more? If Jesus came to reveal God to us, it seems straightforward to say that his death was no more, and no less, than the culmination of his life of self-giving love.

The questions our contemporaries are asking are about how to persist in believing in God, in a self-running universe. They are pressing the objection that Christian faith is pointless, unless Christians can give some definite indication that this loving Creator of theirs exists at all. Christians may reply that faith can live upon quite small indications of God's presence today, provided that they can fill in the meaning of God's love by pointing to the Gospels. In other words, in our time incarnation seems more plainly relevant than atonement.

The life of Christ is an example of what love means: better still, it is the example of what God's love means. The temptation is to take the argument as far as this but no farther. If enquirers want to know what the cross means for us today, it feels more comfortable to moralize than to theologize. So the story of the Man of Sorrows may be told as a bad example of oppression, or as a good example of how to endure suffering: but not as an important or even suitable matter for young Christians to dwell upon, not the heart of our faith.

But the cross *is* the heart of our faith. The way some good human being happened to die may be just an appendix to a biography, added for completeness and introducing a touch of sadness about the shortness of human life. The death of Jesus was never told like this, merely as the last few pages of his story, recounting his eventual unhappy fate. Christians need an understanding of atonement now as much as ever; and there is a way of thinking about the cross which is particularly relevant to the questions of today.

Mild he lays his glory by

We need such a way of thinking, because sceptical doubt takes tougher forms than the agnostic question, 'Is there really enough to go on?' Scepticism moves into atheism when atheism makes a moral stand. Troubled people nowadays, not burdened by sin, are warmly indignant about evil.[1] They look around them at the world, full of pointless suffering, and what they demand is not so much 'Prove God' but 'Face facts: the Creator you say you believe in is a devil.' If Christians suppose that they can protect their children's faith from this kind of attack by keeping quiet about awkward truths, all they do is send their children out into a harsh world unprotected. Fire alarms may be frightening, but they are a lot less frightening than fire.

Christians are confronted by the stern argument that their faith is not merely naive but insensitive: that there is too much wrong with the world for the praise of God to be even proper, still less obligatory. The sting of the problem of evil is that the Creator, if we believe in a Creator at all, is responsible in the last resort for everything that happens. Moralize as we may about sin being worse than evil,[2] sin is human responsibility: evil is God's.

At the risk of seeming irreverent, thoughtful Christians must presume to enquire about God's right to create a world with so much agony in it. They must ask this question more strenuously, not less, when they are trying to hand on their faith to other people, young or old. Once the question has begun to bite, no answer will do which leaves God untouched by the agony. How can a Creator God who is not vulnerable be worshipful?

The Christian God is vulnerable. The God who made the world takes responsibility for it, not only by taking a benevolent interest from on high, but by entering into the world and experiencing at first hand how painful life can be. That is what 'God was in Christ' means. The two natures doctrine, that Jesus Christ was both human and divine, comes to life here. More than that, the doctrine that Christ is God the Son, who existed before his human birth, could come to life too. Some theologians have hoped to put aside his pre-existence as an unnecessary metaphysical theory. They might realize afresh that there is significance in this unfashionable notion: the significance of saying not just 'he lived' but 'he came'.

All this might seem well beyond children's comprehension. What could the vulnerability of God matter until people have reached greater maturity? It matters if it is the answer to real questions. The idea of cheating is well within the comprehension of quite young children. Naturally they will not say, but they are perfectly capable of thinking, that the story of Jesus, on the face of it, is a bit of a cheat. Jesus looked like a real man, but all the time he could see right through everything and everybody, and was never puzzled about what was right or who could be trusted. There was no need for him to worry about dying because he knew that it was all going to come right on Easter Day.[3] What is so very loving about living like that?

Nobody can say about the story of the cross, 'It was all very well for him.' Christ not only faced what the world might do: he faced it as human beings often have to face their troubles, without the comfort of faith. Because God's Son endured God's absence, even the human experience of forsakenness is included in the life of God. The centre of Christian belief is the cry of dereliction 'My God, my God, why hast thou forsaken me?'[4] If any words of Christ recounted in the Gospels are authentic, these are. It is wholly convincing that the words of Psalm 22 should have been running in his head: it is wholly unconvincing that this loss of faith should have been invented. Here if anywhere we 'have the mind of Christ'.[5]

Some Christians worry that the Son of God ought to have died in calm trustfulness. They are tempted, when they have to tell the story of Good Friday, to slide over the cry of dereliction and put the emphasis on the other 'words from the cross'.[6] If they give young Christians the impression that Jesus was really in control all the time, they foster the misunderstanding that God does not truly care about human suffering, only about sin.

It may have seemed irreverent to question God's right to create a world like this, but the question has led straight into the reverence Christian believers owe to the God who paid the price of creating a world like this.[7] There is no halfway house where some sort of respectful approval would be adequate. The God who loved the world enough to come into the world and face whatever the world might do, even death on the cross, is totally worshipful. This is the God in whom Christians put their trust. Once that is said, irreverence vanishes into awe.

On this presumptuous but necessary foundation the more seemly explanations of atonement, of how Christ died for our sins, can be built. Whatever theory we hold about the meaning of his death, he did in fact die as a result of human badness and weakness. People killed him. In that sense he literally 'paid the price of sin'. He bore the brunt of the wrongness which seems to be built into human life.

We are quite used to saying, 'Who but God can forgive sins?',[8] but we can understand the meaning of atonement better if we combine that question with another: 'Who but the victim can forgive sins?' How has anyone who has not been hurt the right to

94

talk about 'reconciliation'? When we have in mind the whole sinfulness of the world, we can see the point of saying, 'It takes God-made-human to forgive.'

On this start we may build an understanding of the death of Jesus, perhaps with the help of theories of atonement which have made sense to earlier Christians: that he was showing God's love to the limit, paying the needful price, rescuing hopeless humanity, winning the victory, or offering the perfect sacrifice. To try to explain some of these ideas in simple words, even in words simple enough for children, far from being an irrelevant exercise, could be the best way to grasp them for oneself.

In earlier centuries people thought naturally in terms of hierarchy. God was king, and what God decreed was not a proper subject for argument. Today people think naturally in terms of democracy and autonomy, and it does not take much courage to admit to oneself, or complain to other people, that the world is dreadfully unfair.[9] When Christians, like their contemporaries, start here, the most illuminating way to think about the cross of Christ is to think of God entering fully into the unfairness. God is not the sort of king who reigns aloft over poor wretches whose troubles belong to their humble estate: God knows at first hand what failure, disappointment, pain, untimely death, and desolation are like.

We cannot assume that our children will never have any troubles. It is up to us to equip them with resources to meet life, however it may turn out for them. 'Whatever happens, God is there' is comfort in the old sense of 'strengthening', which sooner or later they will need.

They need encouragement also to find God's presence in the happiness we hope they will enjoy. The life of Jesus did not consist entirely of 'sorrowing, sighing, bleeding, dying'. It included working and resting, talking and observing, eating and drinking, praying and teaching, helping people and enjoying their company. Ordinariness and celebration can be blessed, as well as crisis and woe, for people who believe that all this is included in the experience of the Lord.

Saying 'God is with us' is the best foundation for saying 'God loves us'. 'Presence' has a practical reality which hasty talk about 'love' can miss. 'Love' is a battered word, which can have many meanings from starry-eyed romance, via emotional blackmail, to hypocrisy. 'I love you,' in the moonlight but not in the kitchen. 'I love my children,' so I spank them for their good. 'I love you,' so you must pay me back in gratitude. 'I love you,' though I am often not available.

People who have been led to regard God's care as available in the kind of way the social services are available may not dare to entertain the thought, 'God doesn't care'; but they may dimly feel that the love of God, like some kinds of human love, is hard to pin down. If it is true that God was in Christ, literally and horribly pinned down, the cross is the pledge that God the Creator is willing to pay the price of creation.

Risen with healing in his wings

Faith, at whatever age, needs to be capable of facing disaster. The good news is not that disaster can be avoided but that Christ has been there and has overcome it. But 'overcome' could be as elusive an idea as 'love'. Since disasters still happen, is it as risky, even dishonest, to tell children that Christ has overcome disaster as it is to affirm that God will always look after us?

The cross is not the whole Christian faith. If it were, the sufferings of Christ, however divine, would remain pointless; and the question what right Christians have to call these sufferings divine would recur in full force. The pattern of Christian hope is cross-and-resurrection: Christ going through failure and vindicated by rising again. Without the cross there could be no atonement, but without the resurrection nobody would know that there was an atonement.

The Christian belief that Jesus rose from the dead is the answer to two questions: Why do you think this human death is a pledge of God's presence? and, What was the good of it? The first Christians bore witness that the cross was not the end of the story, that Jesus came back to them, more alive than ever, and commissioned them to be his ambassadors to the world. From the start they had partly realized that he was more than another prophet; when everything went wrong their hopes crashed; and when he rose from the dead they came to see the story as one whole, and to find the particular presence of God in his life, his death and his rising.

The God Christians worship is the God who is both willing to meet death face to face, and able to overcome death. The Christian faith is about dying to live: finding the best on the other side of the worst. There is no Christianity without courage and hope: courage to face what we fear and hope that beyond fear there is light at the end of the tunnel.[10] If this is explained in simple words, elementary theology need be no more obscure than elementary mathematics, and less frightening than grown-up evasions.

Nothing that human beings want to hold on to can be kept for ever. Childish squabbles and grown-up obsessions tell the same story. It is a recurring pattern in human life that what we grab, we spoil. We cannot conceal from children that however good life is, death comes sooner or later. No gospel that by-passes death is 'gospel truth'. The Christian gospel does not attempt to by-pass death or even make it unimportant. No miraculous help came to save Jesus from the cross. He died and was buried, just as we have to die one day and be buried. It was not 'all very well' for him, and that is why his rising again is 'all very well' for us. Because the miracle did not rescue Jesus from death, being dead does not have to mean 'It's too late'.

The miracle did come, on the other side of death, 'on the third day'. Something happened. How much does it matter that Christians should all speak with one voice about what happened? In the twentieth century even Christians are on edge about miracles, and some would rather play down any suggestion of 'the supernatural' in commending their faith. It does matter to be honest, and part of honesty is 'coming clean': recognizing what doubts we have, and making thoroughly plain what does remain when doubts have been faced.[11]

What should be said first is 'he that is not against you is for you'.[12] Christians have no right to repudiate would-be fellow believers whose faith they judge inadequate. If some followers of Christ think that nothing can have happened to Jesus on the third day, so that the whole meaning of Easter has to be what happened to his disciples, they should not be forbidden to call themselves Christians: though it is hard to see how they claim to have enough to go on.

The natural meaning of 'Jesus rose' is that something did happen to Jesus. There is room for friendly uncertainty about what this means. It might surprise traditional Christians to know how many believers in the resurrection have doubts about the empty tomb. St Paul is our earliest witness, and what he emphasizes, as facts which his readers knew already, is that Jesus died, was buried, was raised on the third day, and appeared to named and known people, including last of all himself.[13] Did St Paul believe that the body they saw was the same physical body which had walked about in Galilee, or a 'spiritual body'[14] such as we all shall have one day in heaven? He does not make this clear.

Some sincere Christians think that the stories that the tomb was found empty are later embellishments. They are right to see difficulties in the seemingly straightforward idea that on Easter Sunday morning the Lord simply got up and walked out. Must it be flippant to enquire what clothes Jesus put on? It is neither flippant nor childish to ask what happened when he bade farewell. In our picture language, he 'ascended into heaven'. Is his physical body still somewhere in the universe? Might astronauts come across it? And if the resurrection of Jesus was something quite different from anything we can hope for after our deaths, how can his rising be the pledge of ours? 'Thou shalt not give thy holy one to see corruption.'[15] Our bodies decay, so we cannot rise in the way Jesus rose. It was all very well for him, after all.

It is not faithless to give weight to all these considerations and let them cast doubt upon the empty tomb. The resurrection can be affirmed, and could be taught to children, without it: yet it seems faint-hearted to give up the wonder of Easter morning too easily. A consideration on the other side is the fundamental Christian conviction that bodies matter. If the Lord's body remained in the tomb, was the Risen Christ a real human being, or a ghost?

There is a way of putting all these difficulties together,[16] which might be a help to anyone who is puzzled but not determined that miracles are out of the question. Our bodies will be naturally and slowly dispersed into the physical world when we die. In the end our tombs will be empty. Suppose the tomb of Jesus was empty already on the third day, not because the body in it was miraculously resuscitated, but because the body in it was miraculously and quickly dispersed into the physical world?

In that case the tomb was indeed empty and the holy one did not 'see corruption'; but not because, unlike us, he kept his earthly body and took it to heaven with him. He was raised in a spiritual body, like the spiritual bodies we hope to have one day. So it makes sense to say that his rising was truly the pledge of our rising. It took a miracle to raise Jesus up, because he was really dead, and it will take a mighty work each to raise us up once we are really dead. The rising of Jesus has shown that mighty works can be done.

12

Finding God in Church

If anyone be in despair . . . let him go joyfully to the Sacrament . . .
and seek help from the entire company of the spiritual body
and say, 'I have on my side Christ's Righteousness, life and
sufferings with all the holy angels and all the blessed in heaven
and all good men upon earth. If I die I am not alone in death. If I
suffer, they suffer with me.'

Martin Luther

Members incorporate[1]

Christ is risen, but we are not risen yet. What means of grace have
we in the meantime? What difference has the life, death and rising
of Jesus Christ made? Part of the answer is the existence of the
Christian church.

The belief that Jesus meant to found the church is unfashionable nowadays: even more unfashionable than the belief that he
was God the Son. We are not in a position to be dogmatic about
his expectations or intentions. Yet his disciples were certainly
bound together in an organization, which theologians have called
the Body of Christ. The persistence of the Christian church is a
fact of history. Two thousand years after Jesus walked in Galilee
the people who belong to this body still believe themselves to be in
touch with him. They happily take possession of St Paul's words,
'Now you are the body of Christ and individually members of it.'[2]
If this answers to our experience, can we tell our children, when
we look around us and fail to locate providence, that God after all
is not absent from the world but is findable 'where two or three
are gathered' in the name of Jesus?[3]

There is no need to imagine that when the Lord called the
Twelve and taught them, he was doing anything in the least like

founding a good cause. The picture of a small group of enthusiasts who set up a committee, draft a constitution, appoint officers, take minutes, register as a charity and proceed to appeal to the public for funds is plainly anachronistic, even though the church has done more or less all those things in his name. There is no need even to suppose that Jesus omnisciently foresaw, with contentment or grief, what his continuing Body would be like. Christians must believe that he sees what is going on now, and hope that he can recognize the church, or more sadly the churches, as representing him as best they can.

Christians have indeed the more lively hope, that after all the Lord is still present among them because they are his people. Their imperfections have not ruled out this hope, any more than the imperfections of God's ancient people could cancel the Covenant. The positive grounding of the belief that God is findable in the church cannot be the church's good record: that is too clear. The church affirms that God is faithful, not that human beings are. What Christians claim is not credit but continuity. So they may go on saying to one another and to their children, 'O taste, and see, how gracious the Lord is.'[4]

The claim is twofold. First, because finding God is always a matter of God's grace not human merit, the church as a human institution need not be wonderful, only adequate, to support the conviction of God's presence. Just as the idea of being 'good enough'[5] has actually encouraged parents to do better, so the idea that God can and does use rough and ready building materials could legitimately hearten Christians who are wondering whether the body they belong to could possibly be the Body of Christ.

Secondly, this conviction that we do not have to depend entirely upon ourselves, far from being a reluctant concession, is the main point of looking in the church for God's presence. It was among the people of God that the psalmist was able to say 'O taste, and see'. In the south transept of Chartres Cathedral the stained glass windows show the evangelists sitting weightily upon the shoulders of the great prophets: a vivid picture of continuity, which is a more telling image of the communion of saints than conventional rows of haloes in heaven. No individual Christian's perception of God's grace has to bear the whole weight, if it is all put into the common pool. What can give a believer today enough to go on is the continuous and cumulative witness of generations.[6] I cannot add a cubit to my stature,[7] but I can sit on the shoulders of St Paul and St Augustine, Julian of Norwich, George Herbert and Thomas Traherne.

Holy fellowship

The Christian church claims continuity with God's people before the coming of Christ. It would be defeatist to look back a long distance to psalmist and prophet, and a shorter distance to Christian saints, and bypass Christ himself. Instead of tangling with the biblical experts about whether or not the Founder founded, there is another way of grounding in the centre of the gospel our conviction of being his people.

Our belonging may turn out to go back more plainly to the death and rising of Christ than to his teaching. Christians ought to be familiar with the idea of God inaugurating a people by means of a great rescue. In the story of the Exodus, it was when the children of Israel were powerless and oppressed that the Lord intervened on their behalf, brought them out of Egypt and fashioned them strenuously into a people. In the gospel story, it was when everything had gone wrong that Jesus rose from the dead and his disorganized disciples became his witnesses. Both stories tell of future hope coming out of immediate gloom.

The Lord on the cross lost touch with the presence of God and cried out in desolation, 'why hast thou forsaken me?'[8] Christians who have worried that such loss of faith might seem unworthy of the Lord have offered the comfortable half truth that Jesus must have been aware of the whole psalm he was quoting, and that the psalm ends not in despair but in hope. If this suggestion is supposed to eliminate the dereliction, it disastrously misses the more realistic comfort: that God in Christ faced, for our sake, the human experience of the absence of God.[9]

But still, Psalm 22 does end with a gleam of light; and it is a fact, not a conjecture, that any boy educated in the synagogue would have been thoroughly familiar with the whole. It is legitimate to remember reverently that the Lord in his extremity,

haunted by the psalmist's desolation, was undergoing an experience that was not going to finish in desolation.[10] We must not
suggest, to our children or to ourselves, that Jesus on the cross
knew clearly that everything was under control and that he would
rise on the third day. But Christians may rightly consider, and be
ready to try to explain, that his despair was contained by an
awareness, maybe an obscure awareness, of belonging to God's
people. He was not the first of God's servants to feel abandoned.
Even in dying, he was part of a tradition. When he cried out that
God had forsaken him, it was to God that he cried out.

So instead of running away from the cry of dereliction,
Christians may use Psalm 22 as a prayer consecrated by the Lord
himself; and in the light of Easter they can go on to take
possession of the last verse of the psalm as well. 'They shall come,
and the heavens shall declare thy righteousness: unto a people
that shall be born, whom the Lord hath made': or, in a newer
translation, 'They shall come and make known to a people yet
unborn the saving deeds that he has done.'[11] It is again a fact, not
a conjecture, that the people who *have been* born, who are still
called by Christ's name, include ourselves. We need not embark
on complex interpretations of what we know about his teaching,
to tell our children that our own membership of God's people
goes back to his membership of God's people, and that our
belonging takes its rise from his death and rising.

Blessed company

But belonging is a tangled concept. If older Christians are
confused about it, the youngest members of the church will enter
into their confusion. There are some tempting muddles here
about the meaning of community, and about what we are to think
of 'the individual'.

It is too easy to move step by step into a tyrannical way of
thinking. The argument starts well. If we can stand on the
shoulders of past Christians, then surely we can and should rely
on the backing of present Christians. Becoming a Christian is
becoming a member of Christ's Body. To try to be a lone disciple
is not merely daunting, it is needless. By the grace of God, we have

a community in which we may live our Christian lives and bring up our children in the knowledge that they belong. So far, so good.

This is where theory and practice begin to come apart. At this rate, the church ought to be the foundation of our lives. For most people, including many firm believers, it plainly is not. How much does the Christian community mean to Western Christian people? Church membership looks like a hobby or a civic duty, or even an insurance policy. If Christians really believed that the church is the Body of Christ, could they possibly be so semi-detached? Is something wrong, and if so, what?

There is a ready answer which is dangerous: not false, but an unsuitable answer to this question. Many good and thoughtful people are telling us that what is wrong with the modern world is 'individualism'.[12] Common life has been fractured into atoms or at best molecules. Some people blame the 'Age of Reason' for the prevalence of a state of mind which counts each person as a separate 'self', each with separate interests to look after. 'All we like sheep have gone astray': not, like sensible sheep, by following the flock, but by turning 'every one to his own way'.[13] If only human beings could understand that we all belong to one another, and stop being so egoistic, so grasping, so set on achievement, so *individualistic*!

This diagnosis of the human condition is the right answer to some questions. Most of us could easily produce evidence for it. We cannot deny, and when we stop to think we mind, that around us there are people who cannot compete, who are pushed aside and left out, the victims, passive or bitter, of everyone else's autonomy. For Christians this indictment is familiar, and we blame ourselves and one another for our failure to get together and do something about it. Though Donne's 'no man is an island' has lost its novelty, it has certainly not lost its relevance.

But 'the community' is not to be idolized any more than 'the self'. When Christians are thinking about political communities they know perfectly well that what starts as 'brotherhood' turns into the tyranny of Big Brother: but they easily jump to the conclusion that the Christian community is different. Surely the church, the Body of Christ, cannot be just another collective which needs watching? Once there was an Inquisition, but not any more. The church is supposed to be the place where we give up our selfish selves and belong to one another.

It is not good enough to get a warm glow from the idea of the Christian community, and assume that the people who have their doubts are selfish or ignorant, needing to be condemned or converted but not heeded. There are indeed selfish people and ignorant people, but there are plenty more who simply feel unconvinced, whatever they think they ought to think. Some of these will conform up to a point, but the message they are receiving and will hand on is about claims laid on us and conditions of membership, not about encouragement and support. Belonging to the Body of Christ looks like a duty or maybe a right, quite different from belonging naturally to the people one really loves.

The need human beings have for community cannot be translated in a hurry into the conviction that the church is God's community and must be our top loyalty. There are a lot of steps missing in the argument. Belonging to the Body of Christ is not a matter of trying to convince ourselves, or our children, that real life is church life, as if all the other doings of our lives hardly counted.

The starting point is still the understanding that we need community. Christians of all people have indeed the right and duty to maintain with confidence that we are bound in one bundle, that we need one another to be ourselves. Human beings are social creatures from birth. Philosophers have sometimes discussed solemnly how anyone can know that there are any 'other minds'.[14] Meanwhile babies smile at their mothers and thrive because they are loved. The idea of 'the individual' as an independent unit who is bound to have difficulty getting in touch with other people is nonsense. There is no question of going back on all this.

This is where C. S. Lewis' principle that the devil 'always sends errors into the world in pairs – pairs of opposites'[15] is relevant as usual. He was discussing this very matter of belonging to one body. 'Individualism' and 'Totalitarianism' were the twin errors he meant. He knew which he thought the worse of the two but made his point by refusing to say.

Offered 'Either/or', C. S. Lewis said 'Neither'. In 1944, when totalitarianism was still the evident enemy, it was startling and salutary to call individualism an error too. Today the balance has shifted. The danger of collectivism has lost its instant urgency, and now the message is that our society is breaking up. Instead of twin errors, we are offered good 'community' threatened by bad individualists. C. S. Lewis' warning against 'Either/or' is still necessary. What we need now is 'Both/and': a good pair of opposites rather than a bad. 'Individual' and 'community' can be distinguished without being opposed.

'Individual' is, and ought to be, a 'hurrah' word as well as a 'boo' word. There is no contradiction here, though it is hard work to keep the picture in focus. People can stand out admirably, or opt out meanly. 'He's a real individualist' tells us that he has an interesting character. It does not say anything, either way, about whether he is selfish or unselfish. We may be sorry that he is so uncooperative or glad that he is a stout nonconformist. 'She loves them all as individuals' is not at all incompatible with 'They are a close-knit community.'

People who have understood that achievement is not everything, that competitiveness has victims, and that one person's success can be another person's failure, can explain all this just as clearly if they like individuals as they can if they deplore them. 'Cherish every one of God's children. Every single one is special.' Each one of us matters to God, and that includes 'I matter to God.'[16] The false gospel of 'I'm no good' is a recipe for droopy inadequacy or priggishness, not for Christian love.

Christians today should keep their heads and insist, against the fashion, that there is a proper individualism which has to do with the value of human beings. We need this corrective. There is a false equation about, which comes from carelessly adding up three facts: people need community; selfish people opt out; the church is the community where we can set about finding God together. All these statements are true, but they do not justify a one-sided idealism about the church as a human institution. Communities can be overweening too. When some people are put off, they are accused of selfish individualism. They may feel guilty or rebellious or both, but in any case the people of God will be the poorer.

Eastern Orthodox Christians have an answer: to distinguish the *individual* from the *person*.[17] The individual grabs: the person learns what it means to give. Individuals are isolated interchangeable units: persons are unique, precious and related to one another. That could be a more useful terminology than ours; but unfortunately our ambivalence is embedded in our language and we are most unlikely to get rid of it. We speak both well and ill about individuals and will have to make the best of it. Moralists might try saying 'atomism' to make it clear when they are talking about the kind of bad individualism which turns in upon oneself and destroys community. Sorting out muddles can begin to clear the ground for approaching the real question about how God can be found and how the body of people who are called by the name of Christ can help.

Mystical body

The church is like the tip of an iceberg. It is the part of the communion of saints which we can meet directly. People who belong to the church now are the representatives of the whole Body. Their job is formidable but not lonely.

It can always be said that Christians are inadequate representatives. Most of us can think of plenty of criticisms of the church as we know it. Friendly criticism needs to be voiced, or responsible people are left at the mercy of unfriendly criticism or deafening silence.

Friendly criticism is appreciative, realistic and specific. It starts with gratitude and goes on to clarify misunderstandings. The church where one belongs is the church one can criticize best. A Christian who belongs happily to the Church of England has a lot to be grateful for, and on that basis can notice some threatening hindrances, which mostly arise from people not seeing one another's points of view.

Most seriously, the church is widely perceived as rejecting human mercy, generosity and good sense. The opposite of 'liberal' is not 'traditional' but 'illiberal', and there is enough illiberalism about to scare off people of goodwill and make them disinclined to belong to such a body or encourage their children to join it. The more some well-meaning clergy, anxious to do their duty, try to 'uphold standards', the more lay people see with sinking hearts that their thinking friends and relatives are being effectively driven out.

Polite indifference is more prevalent than hostility, and hardly less of a hindrance. It is the bad side of a blessing, that English people are not much prone to anti-clericalism. They therefore tolerate what they see as the pointless preoccupations of the clergy, and refrain from letting the vicar know their own preoccupations. No doubt they are a little nervous of the vicar's disapproval; but they are still more afraid of being rude or unkind.

So incomprehension smothers goodwill. Church life and ordinary life come apart, and clerical and lay Christians begin to speak different languages. Language which is supposed to describe the church is particularly apt to go quietly adrift without anyone saying 'Help! I can't understand this.'

To St Paul it meant a lot to call the church the Body of Christ and Christians members of his Body.[18] The very success of this image has weakened it for later Christians. 'Membership' has lost its fresh metaphorical force, and has nothing much to do with hands or feet which are living parts of an organism. Being a member of an organization is not generally a particularly exacting kind of belonging. Children join clubs with more or less enthusiasm, and become Brownies or support wild life or study computers. Their clothes are covered with badges which proclaim assorted identifications. Their elders pay their subscriptions, likewise with more or less enthusiasm. After a while interest fades and nobody particularly minds, though there may be some nagging on the lines of 'You say you have nothing to do and you haven't even opened that magazine you used to like so much.' Belonging is fun or boring, and joining and lapsing is part of growing up. On the face of it the church looks like another club and has its keen members who keep it going and its casual members who float in and out. When you float out, the nagging starts, not always from the keen members but from the ones who feel insecure about other people's freedom.

If the church is not just a club with a large keen membership, what is it? The image of the family of God has still greater authority than the image of the Body of Christ. The conviction that God is Father is at the heart of the teaching of Jesus. It follows that human beings are brothers and sisters. Christians have always taken this application to heart, at least with their fellow Christians. The message is more telling than the vague and idealistic notion of 'the brotherhood of man', which flattens out the gospel into a slogan. The early Christians had a lively experience of being almost literally a family.

When the church is widespread and is not being persecuted the image becomes a metaphor, more or less vivid. Today the idea of the church as a family has plenty of vitality in it; but because it means different things to different people it can give trouble. When church people use this image to make claims rather than to shed light, it may seem like part of the problem, not part of the answer.

'When you are baptized, you become a member of a new family.' According to the form for the Baptism of Children in the Alternative Service Book, these words are to be said to children who are 'old enough to understand'. If they were taken to heart they could sound quite threatening. A shy child, for whom it is already a formidable enterprise to deal with the two worlds of home and school, will not be at all encouraged by yet another set of people making huge demands. More probably all the children present will realize that this is another example of grown-up language which does not mean anything in particular. There are often a good many children at christenings. If a Christian congregation makes these announcements about the church being their family without really knowing what they mean, they are sowing seeds of polite unreality which will flower later in distrustful disengagement from all things ecclesiastical.

It is hopeless to try to hand on ideas which are not grounded in human reality. People who find family life satisfying know perfectly well that the church patronal festival does not begin to mean as much to them as their children's birthdays. People whose family lives are in disarray are disheartened by being told that in church they can find more of the same. People who have chosen to lead unconventional lives are quite ready to find their suspicion borne out that Christians are judgmental and smug.

It is more likely that Christians are muddled. Church life at its best is indeed like family life at its best. But family life, even at its best, is not sacrosanct. To idealize family life is not particularly Christian, and we are told that Jesus had some hard things to say about families.[19] If to the shaky assumption that 'the family' is holy we add the equally shaky assumption that a church becomes a family just by saying so, we have the makings of idolatry.

It is a shame to spoil the image of the family, because it is one of the best ways of illustrating the true character of Christian life.[20] There are parishes where people who worship together enter into each other's joys and sorrows and find themselves truly part of the family of God. This is how things ought to be: but it happens by careful nurturing, not by presumption. Anyone who talks about church life as family life ought to ask the question, 'Am I describing or moralizing?' and if 'moralizing' is the answer, give the family image a rest for a bit. There are other ways for God's children to encourage one another.

13

Belonging

'Hearken thou to the supplications of thy servant and of thy people Israel when they pray toward this place; yea, hear thou in heaven thy dwelling place; and when thou hearest, forgive.

Prayer of King Solomon (II Chron. 6.21)

Assist us with thy grace

The church is there to make God findable.[1] This is not just an old-fashioned way of saying that members of Christian congregations make God's world a better place for one another. Being a warm-hearted community is not the whole story. What people ask of the church, or anyway what they should ask, is to put them in touch with God.

'Togetherness' can become a substitute for seeking God together. We might reverse a saying of Voltaire[2] and say that the good can be the enemy of the best. The church's proper role is to be the carrier of many centuries of Christian experience. Each Christian congregation, indeed each Christian, represents the whole communion of saints; and 'represent' is a strong word with a definite meaning. To belong to the church is to be able to draw upon resources far beyond one's own. Whatever God's people in earlier generations have discovered is made available for God's would-be people now.

The church should not claim to be the only place for finding God. God is perfectly able to bypass the 'proper channels' and get in touch with human beings in what conventional believers may think of as unorthodox ways. The church should claim to be the place where we do not have to do everything for ourselves, where worship is going on and we may join in. At the beginning of Morning and Evening Prayer in the Book of Common Prayer, the minister says, 'I pray and beseech you . . . to accompany me . . . unto the throne of the heavenly grace.' This is an invitation to approach God in one another's company. For people who are able to accept the invitation, the church is a 'means of grace'.

The practical reality looks different. There is no need to bandy statistics. Perhaps Sunday is still 'special': but not because it is the day for coming together to worship God. On the contrary, religious observance is seen as a kind of compulsion the devout seem to feel. Churchgoing has become a specialized activity, quite virtuous in itself but not much to do with real life.

Christians inside churches are shielded from what is going on outside. To clergy and to people in pews the diagnosis is simple enough: 'They all with one accord began to make excuse.'[3] Strenuous believers are inclined to add, 'So, because you are lukewarm, and neither cold nor hot, I will spew you out of my mouth.'[4] Dutiful churchgoers, in their obedient conformity, can hardly see how much they themselves are part of the problem. They are communicating a picture of God as an aged relative who is easily offended, whom they are required to visit on Sundays. If more people, young and old, are going to find in church God's grace to live by, some rethinking will have to be done.

The problem cannot be solved in terms of duties fulfilled or unfulfilled, when really it is a problem of needs met or unmet. The majority who say they believe in God but absent themselves from public worship are too easily lumped together as idle. Human beings are more variegated than that and their spiritual states are harder to fathom.

There are many stages in people's lives when they have an inkling that ordinary reality is not all there is, that there is something more which believers call 'grace'; but ordinary reality is so demanding that they never manage to explore what grace might mean. Being a parent of young children could be a particularly promising stage for finding heavenly meaning, if only there were time to find anything. In the section of the Book of Common Prayer called 'Forms of prayer to be used at sea' there is a little heading, 'Short prayers for single persons, that cannot meet to join in Prayer with others, by reason of the Fight, or Storm'. Though one hopes that family life when children are young is not exactly a fight, it certainly has the aspect of a storm. Common prayer is meant to be a support. How can that support be offered more realistically?

Humanly speaking, it is unrealistic to expect a mother with several small children of assorted ages to attend to eternal verities, still less to look upon church membership as a live option. The whole thing just looks too difficult for her.[5] She is already overtired and struggling to get done what has to be done: getting children up in the morning, off to school, fed, organized, helped, encouraged, warned, protected, amused, put to bed, got up again next day, and so on apparently for ever. Must Sunday be a day with as rigid a timetable as any other? Her next priority would be a rest, maybe a holiday with her husband, not added religious duties whose point is not obvious.

What this means is that her children are learning, from their babyhood, that belonging to God's people is not for them. She may or may not teach them to call themselves Christian, but she is implanting in their minds the lesson that church is for the others, the righteous ones with time on their hands.

This diagnosis is gloomy, but there is more hope in it than wringing one's hands over the 'uncommitted'. In the children's tug-of-war game called Nuts in May the children sing 'Who shall we send to fetch her away?' and one chosen child tries to pull another into line. If Christian congregations could get rid of the Nuts in May mentality and stop asking unrealistically, 'How can we bring these people in?' they might begin to ask the more constructive question, 'How can we carry them?' Unchurched people at present, and their children, have too little reason to believe that the Christian community is on their side. There is a long way to go: but replacing frowns by smiles would make a start.

Good people who would hate to be intolerant easily fall into the 'two standards' trap. 'I am called upon to serve God: you are let off.' What they should be saying is, 'I am called, at the moment, to serve God in this way.' Christians in pews, after all, do not particularly want to believe that they are the good ones, and that the others are useless until they are folded in. Suppose devoutness really is what it looks like, a specialized calling.

Christians who are able to give time to churchgoing would surely find it more comfortable not to have to see themselves as 'the pick of the bunch'. What they are is representatives, not better, not worse, but entrusted with a two-way task: offering praise and receiving grace on behalf of other people as well as themselves.

Christians readily imagine that devoutness ought to be catching, which is a quick route to discouragement. Plenty of Christian families, including vicarage families, have learnt the hard way that strenuous piety may not set the kind of 'good example' which brings the others in. On the contrary, when some people have a clear vocation they are expected to carry the load. That is what being a representative means. Pious Christians can learn at first hand one way of 'bearing one another's burdens'.[6] Instead of tormenting themselves with blame, they can allow themselves to appreciate fellow human beings outside the fold who are just as virtuous, just as important, and just as beloved, as the ones who happen to be inside. 'If these non-churchgoers are special to me, how much more are they special to God' is no heresy: it ought to be a plain lesson.

'Represent' is still a strong word. Its meaning goes both ways. A representative is an intermediary. To receive something on behalf of the others is to be responsible for conveying it to them. If the 'core' people could stop separating themselves from the 'fringe' people, whether to ignore, to blame, or even to excuse, they might set about meeting their needs. The false clarity of the 'out' and 'in' distinction is bedevilling the whole question. God's grace can be found in church like lava can be found in a volcano. If the lava stayed put, the volcano would be extinct.

All faithful people

What is actually happening as a result of Christian good intentions? Inflexible conditions for coming in and undemanding permission to stay out are alike in conveying the message 'You are not real members of our Body.' Either way, people are left out of the communion of saints where they might find resources of faith and grace.

Many people find a way in to faith by latching on to the faith of other people, drawing upon their long-term small-scale positive experience. If the strongest arguments for the truth of Christianity are cumulative,[7] belonging to the communion of saints can be intellectually important, not just emotionally soothing. It is hard for non-joiners to give the arguments a chance to accumulate. People who feel that integrity demands full conviction before they can take up membership are deprived of this promising and proper way of being convinced. At least their number should not be swollen by people who feel themselves unwelcome.

A fine prayer of the Eastern Church begins, 'Be mindful, O Lord, of thy people present here before thee, and of those who are absent through age, sickness or infirmity.'[8] Christians in church pray heartily for the members of the flock who are undergoing tribulations. They do pray too for God's children who for all sorts of reasons, good and bad, are not members of the flock. Could they pray for them in a more friendly way, taking human concerns as much to heart as churchy concerns? Could 'committed' Christians take the faith of semi-detached parishioners seriously by sometimes asking for their prayers? 'Say one for me' is apt to be a sheepish acknowledgment that worldliness lacks something. It could be used in reverse as an honest acknowledgment that churchiness lacks something.

Believers are uncomfortable with people who call themselves Christian without coming to church. There is a lot of vague guilt about, and it is easy enough to exacerbate it while keeping one's own conscience clear. Of course it looks more loyal to accuse fringe believers of trifling with God, making up their own religion, picking and choosing what they happen to fancy. The Christian faith, indeed, is not for us to invent; but this truth needs to be held together with the truth the fringe believers see, that what goes on in church is not the whole of our faith nor the whole of our lives.

We have a Decade of Evangelism: lay people are being exhorted to witness to their faith. They have a more immediate duty: to tell the clergy, with courtesy, how things look to lay people. It is necessary to explain the shocking foolish fact that the Body of Christ can look like an unwelcoming in-group. The tale may be so elementary as to be trivial, but the alternative is cruel: first polite cotton wool, and then blame for failing to understand.

An unpalatable fact which needs to be faced is that many lay people simply assume that church services will be more or less boring. If they go to church, they go for the sake of obedience. If they feel able to let themselves off, they happily stay away. Once upon a time the likely dreariness of Sunday worship cast no doubt upon its rightness, because most people, and especially children, expected to be bored for a good deal of the time anyway. But nowadays church attandance seems to stick out as something required of believers 'to glorify God' with the implication that God is well glorified by boredom.

Lay people, who can see where the shoe pinches, have a duty to voice this kind of difficulty, at the risk of being misunderstood. Does God always prefer certain repeated rituals to all the other good things people might otherwise be doing? A Christian who joins in a family outing on a Sunday may feel poised between celebration and disapproval. Is it disloyal not to want these children, playing boisterous games with their human father, to be tidied up and made to sit still, listening to words 'hard to be understood'[9] in honour of their heavenly Father? Does God really want us all cooped up indoors for about an hour every Sunday uttering ritual words? If such a God is not only unattractive but incredible, no wonder 'divine service' is widely treated as obsolete.

We are told, 'If they cared enough they would come. They take the trouble to get their children to school on time.' School is different because it is plainly compulsory. The options are 'Come punctually, with all the others; or be in trouble.' The church options are 'Come punctually, into this strange milieu; or avoid embarrassment and maybe try again some other day.' If 'some other day' never comes, the next generation is doubly cut off, with no memories of seemly Sundays long ago to give them the sense that after all they do belong.

Are we to water down what happens in church to make it more appealing? The danger is evident: brief bright services may lose all sense of mystery and leave everybody undernourished, while still not attracting many outsiders. Making people welcome once they have begun to feel unwelcome is not so easy. Neither bribing nor nagging is the answer. Could *some* churches try a different plan, not short simplified services, where everyone is supposed to feel at home, but more spacious celebrations of God's glory, something like the older Good Friday pattern? When people are encouraged to join in for a little while, they often find themselves staying for the whole. In some cathedrals where many visitors come there are prayers every hour as a reminder that this is a holy place. The benefits may be invisible, but should be weighed against the equally invisible damage of 'all or nothing'.

Of course 'drop-in' churchgoing is unworthy of God: but no churchgoing whatever does not even make a beginning. Could we find a way of consecrating the Sunday at home or the day out, by welcoming God's children older or younger into church, even briefly, to ask for a blessing or to say thank you? Indeed, to be honest, that is what the most dedicated Sunday observance really is. Of course we do not give God what we owe. We give a little to represent and consecrate the whole.[10] It would make more sense to teach children 'God wants this chance to bless us in all our doings', rather than 'God likes prayers and hymns and doesn't think much of fun.'

The distinction between 'committed' and 'uncommitted' must be dangerous for young Christians. There is a humbler and more promising way of characterizing people of all ages who are definitely trying to follow Christ: they are *practising*[11] their faith. We are told to be perfect,[12] and practice makes perfect. Beginners practising a musical instrument will tinkle or squawk untunefully, and repeat the elementary exercises intolerably. If one day we are to make heavenly music together we shall have to be patient with one another while we learn.

Being patient is easier if we can positively honour, not just tolerate, one another's different vocations. There is a question of integrity: the integrity of the seeker who cannot say 'Yes' unthinkingly. For some people, much of what goes on in church is hardly honest. For others, a good deal of extrovert contemporary Christianity is showing off, 'praying on street corners'.[13] Instead of nagging and disapproval, they need ways in which they, and their children, can find the grace of God. Seekers and shy people are God's children. It may be hard for ministers, who need to be confident and fairly extrovert if they are to be happy in their work, not to see caution as idleness and shyness as unfriendliness.

Reticence is to be respected, not confused with cowardice. Privacy is not to be insensitively infringed in the name of the Father who sees in secret.[14] The church is where Christians need not be lonely, not where they are forbidden to be quiet.

If this is 'folk religion', so be it. All the Gospels suggest that it is characteristic of the Lord to operate at the fuzzy edges of institutional religion, among the crowd 'who do not know the law'.[15] When the church today has fuzzy edges there is no necessity to diagnose worldliness. A church with strict boundaries is like a house with a burglar alarm: anyone unscrupulous enough will probably find a way to break in, but honest people who have mislaid the key are defeated. 'No hurdles' is a wiser slogan.[16]

Heirs through hope

The first step in meeting the needs of people on the edges, and their children, is to take seriously the idea that God takes them seriously. They do not need to be made over into someone else's pattern: they do need ways of keeping in touch with the communion of saints. Because human beings are embodied, 'in touch' has to have a literal meaning. Physical creatures need physical 'means of grace': that is, ways of giving spiritual realities an earthly shape. Fringe belonging, even more than mainstream belonging, needs to express itself sacramentally, in this wide sense: with traditional ceremonies, Christmas carols, harvest pumpkins, wedding bells, even Easter eggs. People who practise 'folk religion' know this perfectly well and fight a sad battle with possessive 'committed Christians' to be allowed welcoming access to known ways of finding grace.[17]

The test case is baptism. Here, of all places, Christians plausibly claim the right to be possessive. Baptism is a great sacrament. How can we dare to debase it by sentimentally going along with any young parents who want an excuse for a party? The logic is clear enough but the practical effect is alarming.

Once upon a time there was no problem about 'indiscriminate' baptism. It was urgent to baptize all babies, because without baptism you could not get into heaven, and as soon as you committed any sins at all you were liable to go to hell. Now Christians are less sure what baptism is; and several good ways of thinking are converging to make a problem.

Since we are still convinced that baptism is important, we need a fresh account of it, and there is one ready to hand. Baptism, surely, is the sacrament of belonging, just as the eucharist is the sacrament of nourishment. It is the way a new Christian becomes 'a member of Christ, the child of God, and an inheritor of the kingdom of heaven'.[18] But then, how can one ask for membership without wanting to be a member? So, with church approval, more and more children are to grow up unbaptized. Not only heedless parents but some of the most honourable are unwilling to commit themselves. However good the logic, the message for their children is clearer than ever: 'Christianity is not for the likes of us.' The less ferocious understanding of baptism does not damn the unbaptized, but shows them all the same a less welcoming face.

Meanwhile the churches have been making ecumenical progress. Since we all have one baptism, we can recognize one another as Christians. People in other churches truly belong. On the one hand this represents a triumph: on the other hand it creates an exclusiveness of its own. More people are in; but the ones outside are more out than ever.

Some conscientious Christians are suggesting that, rather than profane the sacrament of baptism, the church ought to offer a service of naming, thanksgiving and blessing for the babies of people who do not really want to join. But what is such a service supposed to do for these children, who are not to be made members of Christ's Body?[19] Are they in or out? What kind of blessing is this, which is to be provided as a second best instead of the full-scale welcome reserved for the babies of the committed?

Of course there is a good deal to be said for believers' baptism. If nobody were to be christened as a baby, the 'in' and 'out' distinction need not apply to children at all. They would have a real option to join when they were old enough. But if it seems good that Christian children should be included in the Body of Christ from babyhood,[20] the choice is 'indiscriminate' baptism or difficult discrimination. The logic of strictness must be respected, but if it defeats Christian understanding something is going wrong.

What is going wrong is that the parents not the baby are being judged. Do they fulfil certain conditions? Have they attended enough services? Have they been properly instructed? Can they go along with current ideas about what makes a suitable welcome for a new Christian? Are they willing to fit in with the way things are done in this parish, and leave out of account the enthusiasim, not to mention the convenience, of their own family and friends, this baby's nearest community?

To take baptism seriously is not to hedge it about with conditions but to ask what is really going on. As soon as it looks as if God's grace is conditional upon anyone's worthiness we have gone astray. The candidate is the baby not the parents. We are asking God to enrol this small human being as a Christian. Of course we are asking a lot and perhaps we do not altogether know what we ask. Prayers may be answered in unexpected ways.

Rigorists, trying to avoid the risk of taking God's name in vain, give the impression of knowing too well what we ought to ask. Even their emphasis that baptism is the sacrament of belonging seems to set human limits to what belonging can mean. They seem to assume too easily that belonging to Christ is the same thing as belonging to a human institution.

People who bring a baby for baptism are doing something to make way for God's grace. Humanly speaking, they are at least laying a foundation for a future time when the question will arise for this child whether the Christian faith is a live option. It is worth saying bluntly to rigorists: if they say No, the responsibility for rebuffing a child of God is theirs; if they say Yes, it is the child's family who take upon themselves the responsibility for honouring or dishonouring God's name.

This argument is bound to sound dangerous because it seems to weaken the essential connection between baptism and faith. When the candidate for baptism is an infant, who has to do the believing? Surely people who bring a baby to the font must be recognizable Christians? So 'commitment', by somebody, seems to count for more than care for this particular baby. It is all natural and logical, and still the message is that only conformists are acceptable to God.

Could Christians dare to say that the faith which qualifies is simply enough faith to ask God to take on this child? The theology of this is simple, but sounder than ardent parishioners might think. When we try to explain what baptism means, we may emphasize washing away sin, or joining a body; but the basic meaning of baptism is becoming a Christian. St Paul called baptism 'putting on Christ'.[21] Fringe believers want their baby christened. The church is there to help. There are three principles: that nobody is worthy; that asking does seriously mean asking; and that what God gives, and what God will one day ask, may turn out to be more than we now realize. A new Christian is signed with the cross, in the name of Christ who died and rose again. We are not dealing in 'cheap grace'.

If a pious home, faithful godparents, well-instructed parents, or a welcoming congregation are lacking, the Christian nurture of this child will be difficult, but it is not for us to say that God is not even to be asked to enrol a new Christian. It follows that twentieth-century liturgical revision, in trying to get away from the Prayer Book emphasis on human sinfulness, has taken an unfortunate turning. The form for the Baptism of Children in the Alternative Service Book puts so much stress on belonging to the family of the church, and on the commitment of the parents and godparents, that it ought to scare off more people than it does, forbidding an honest welcome for waverers. Strangely enough, in the Rite A communion service the congregation say 'We believe', which may sound like putting the load upon other people's shoulders; whereas in asking for baptism on behalf of a baby, in dependence upon the faith of the whole church, everyone has to say 'I believe' or keep awkwardly silent. It does not follow that the revisers have got it right.

Nor does it follow that the required setting for baptism must be the parish eucharist, unfamiliar and frightening to unaccustomed worshippers. It is still less apparent that the hopes and expectations of an older generation must be an unworthy reason for christening the new baby. The dismissive 'It's only to please the grandmother' forgets how Russian Orthodox Babushkas, we are told, have played their part in keeping the Christian faith from succumbing to atheism.

Most of these difficulties come from treating belonging as an end in itself instead of a means to an end. The end is for people, young and old, to be enabled to get in touch with God. Members of the Body of Christ can support one another in their search and encourage one another in their finding. In many churches this really happens. We can tell our children that the Christian life is something which is going on anyway. To join is like stepping on to a roundabout. The notion that religion is 'the flight of the alone to the Alone' is deeply alien to Christianity. We can say to one another, 'Won't you join the dance?'[22]

As soon as pious believers mainly make demands, especially on new Christians, rather than setting about meeting their needs, as soon as belonging becomes a condition rather than a privilege, we have the makings of tyranny. The church needs the two emphases, which might be caricatured as Catholic and Protestant, on the communion of saints and on individual integrity. Catholic-minded Christians are grateful for the support of fellow Christians past and present. Protestants are careful to remember that our responsibility is to God not to human intermediaries. It is best when these attitudes characterize the same people.

14

Finding God in the Bible

The Pauline letters are letters from St Paul to the churches, not
letters from God to St Paul.

James Barr[1]

Written for our learning[2]

Clergy worry about non-joiners. Surely it must be a sign of failure
if the flock declines, however politely, to be a flock? When people
refuse to be committed, are they endangering their souls and the
souls of their children? This anxiety reckons too little with the
honourable Protestant suspicion of 'churchiness'. Lay people,
especially those who call themselves 'C of E', tend to believe deep
down that each of us has a direct line to God and should not
depend upon intermediaries, even ordained intermediaries. The
saying 'Call no man your father upon earth'[3] seems less baffling
when it is half-consciously interpreted, 'Don't call the vicar
Father.'

Can these Protestant Christians find God in the Bible? They are
not steeped in it any more and nor will their children be; but
somehow or other they still feel that Holy Scripture is the real
authority. Even among people who are not too sure whether a
famous quotation comes from the Bible or Shakespeare, or what
is the difference between the Ten Commandments and the
Golden Rule, there is the residual conviction that the Bible is the
place where God is to be found, maybe as a last resort. What is in
the Bible is what Christians are expected to believe. It may be
tacitly added, 'So never mind what the church says.'

The mistake is to take the Bible apart from the church.[4] We
have the Bible from the church. The Bible puts us in touch with
God, not without intermediaries, but through God's people who

have been aware of God's presence. The inspiration of the Bible is no less real for being complex. The simple appeal 'The Bible says' fails to appreciate how closely the authority of the Bible and the authority of our tradition are intertwined.

Protestant Christians can read the Bible for themselves, but none the less depend upon other people at all points. The Bible was written, copied, translated by people: and it needs to be interpreted by people. Those of us who are not biblical scholars should have a lively expectation of help, not hindrance, from those who are. The help we have had recently includes reminders that the Bible is a library of variegated teaching, not one monochrome book.[5]

Reading the Bible, just as much as belonging to the church, is a way of finding God by way of the communion of saints. Fundamentalists by-pass the communion of saints: as if the Bible were the exact equivalent of the Koran. Likewise, at the other end of the spectrum, severely radical critics also cut modern Christians off from the Christians of the past: as if we could not enter at all into ancient ways of thinking. Fundamentalists see secretaries taking dictation. Radicals see human authors whose notions belong entirely to their own day. Either way, the fellow believers to whom we owe our faith are under-estimated.

When it comes to handing on the gospel, it is the critical point of view which oddly enough goes by default. Because radicals are supposed to be more sophisticated than fundamentalists, they may feel that to have a missionary spirit about radicalism is neither necessary nor desirable. People who aspire to sophistication are sometimes quite protective of other people, especially young ones, and nervous of destroying their innocence. Are these little ones strong enough to take it if they are told about problems which have not so far occurred to them?

Carefully chosen verses from the Bible are read in church and the congregation is told, 'This is the word of the Lord.' How ungrateful to refuse to join in the response, 'Thanks be to God.' So the seeds of literal-mindedness are widely sown. To certify particular passages of the Bible, out of context, as God's direct speech strongly suggests that the letter is the place to find the Spirit.

Fundamentalists encourage, and radicals fail to tackle, a notion of 'Holy Scripture' which lives in a separate compartment from reason, commonsense and experience. Grown-ups with very different notions of biblical inspiration find it less trouble to teach children 'Bible stories', only vaguely related to everything else they are expected to learn and believe, than to complicate their lives by pointing out the difficulties.[6] The dogmatism of the fundamentalist, 'You must believe this without asking questions', converges with the defeatism of the radical, 'There's no point in asking what really happened.' People of all ages who mind about discovering the truth are hampered either way.

Children are small human beings, capable of rational thought. They can understand the difference between truth and lies. Nor need the gentler distinction between fact and fiction be beyond them, nor the idea of a mistake; but because they begin by trusting the grown-ups, they can easily be deceived and they can easily be muddled. Are Bible stories really true, true in the real world?

'Don't tell stories' is another way of saying, 'Don't tell fibs.' When children are frightened by something they have read they have probably been comforted, 'Don't worry: it's only a story.' That 'only' remains when the particular occasion has long ago been forgotten. 'Story' wobbles somewhere between 'fable' and 'history', just as 'myth' in most people's minds hovers on the edge of the mythical. This built-in difficulty could partly spoil the refreshing emphasis on 'narrative' which characterizes some of the most positive biblical scholarship today.[7]

Comfort of the scriptures[8]

When children or grown-ups ask questions about how to understand the Bible, the 'Word of the Lord' is put to the test. 'Why doesn't Jesus make Aunt Mary better?' 'Are there real devils?' 'Ought women to obey men?' 'What does the Bible say about abortion?' People who have been led to suppose that God speaks to us directly naturally expect instant illumination. It is no wonder that they bandy texts and make debating points: or that when they are disappointed they stop treating the Bible as inspired at all.

Illumination used to be a good image for understanding: before people could expect electric light at the flick of a switch, when houses were dark in the evenings, candles were expensive, and the dawn came slowly. A better image today is nourishment. Nobody would expect starving children to grow plump and vigorous on one hefty meal. Nor should people who are spiritually starved be expected to grow into understanding on a diet of biblical pronouncements served up to them out of context. If Christians are to be nourished by the Bible they need to keep on reading it, not in snippets but as a whole. This is not because scripture is really all of a piece, but just because it is variegated and complex.

If we hope to discover 'the mind of Christ'[9] in the Bible we must give ourselves the chance to be sustained by the multiple resources of the whole, rather than relying on proof-texts as a sort of quick snack. We can be grateful for the company of the communion of saints present and past. It is true that many of our predecessors seem to have understood the Bible in ways which are alien to us now, pre-critically literal or artificially allegorical. They had never heard of source criticism, form criticism, redaction criticism or narrative criticism: but their minds were steeped in these books and the love of God is able to come through. Gregory of Nyssa writing the Life of Moses or Augustine preaching on the psalms were not stuck with the letter but could put their fellow Christians in touch with the spirit.

If twentieth-century Christians nourish themselves upon the Bible, using all the help they can get from one another, what sustenance is there for them? In other words, what convictions about God will characteristically grow in the minds of people who feed upon this long-term diet?

Two themes are especially worth picking out: not, of course, because they are the whole story, but because they are basic, neglected, and particularly suitable for introducing beginners to the Christian faith. The main theme ought to be obvious: *God is not an idol*. The second theme, which needs to be set free from the layers of smothering moralism, is the idea of generous *welcome*.

The God who surprises

God is 'the high and lofty One that inhabiteth eternity, whose name is Holy'.[10] God cannot be domesticated. There is a question-mark against the kind of piety which does not allow for God's strangeness. Human beings make a huge mistake when they imagine themselves as God's courtiers with the entrée to the audience chamber, who know what is going on and hope for a say in the royal policy.

Trusting God is different from taking God for granted. People who worship an idol can consciously or unconsciously put words into their God's mouth. They may loyally maintain the tradition, but they are not likely to learn anything new. The God who is not an idol has surprises in store for human beings. The divine message is often, 'Not like that: like this.'

It is defeatist, and indeed self-defeating, to try to teach children about the Christian faith and leave out its paradoxical quality. Children are no more likely than grown-ups to be inspired by a bland God who is predictably comprehensible. Dutiful respect for a heavenly headmaster-figure who is kind, or stern, or with luck merciful, who is there in the last resort to sort out their problems, is all very well but has not much to do with worship.

There are resources in the library of books we call the Bible for more adventurous explorations. Of course there has to be selection. It is tempting to leave out the bloodthirsty God of Joshua, though honesty suggests that suppression is not the answer. A long-term look at the gradual education of a people could stand us all in better stead. At least children could have a change from Noah's Ark with the animals obediently queuing up and most of the human beings drowning inconspicuously in the background.

Jonah's surprising adventure has always been a favourite. People who no longer readily see Jonah's third-day escape as a preview of the resurrection[11] still enjoy making pictures of sea-monsters. They need not leave out the end of the story: Jonah, hot and cross, sulking outside Nineveh, and God sparing the city and teasing the prophet.

Must grown-ups foster the conviction, foreign to scripture,

that God classifies every human being tidily as a 'goody' or a 'baddy'? Once that notion has put down roots it is as hard to eradicate as dandelions; but quite young children are capable of being intrigued and indeed enlightened by the idea that reality is not so straightforward. Ian Ramsey[12] used to talk about 'disclosures', when light dawns, the penny drops, and something is revealed which transcends ordinary expectation. The disclosure that God's holiness is not moralistic crops up all over the Bible, if only it is not timidly censored.

The history of David, the ideal king of God's people, is all the more impressive when it is told with the paradoxes and tragedy mixed up with the greatness and triumph.[13] It would be a shame not to look squarely at David's simultaneous loyalty and rivalry to King Saul; his qualities of leadership, and especially his inspiring but near-manipulative generosity, which put in the shade the unequivocal generosity of Jonathan who was not chosen;[14] his agonized lament for Saul and Jonathan in his hour of victory;[15] his sin with Bathsheba and his repentance;[16] his failure over his son Absalom;[17] and indeed the limitations of the glorious kingdom he established.

There need be no temptation to censor the story of David. It can be told as a moral tale, though not a platitudinous one. The story of Jacob is evidently more recalcitrant. If people have to be counted as goodies and baddies, then Jacob by most standards was a baddy. Is his standing as a patriarch a blemish on our tradition? On the contrary, if David's story can be an introduction to the complexity of human glory, Jacob's story could be an introduction to the complexity of the glory of God.[18]

What Jacob wants is the blessing. He cheats his brother and their aged father for it; and proceeds to prosper exceedingly. When eventually he has to face Esau it is hardly surprising that for all his cleverness and success he is afraid, aware that it would serve him right if God rejected him.[19] So far, so moral.

The story does not go the way a child's sense of justice might expect; but children whose sense of justice has not yet hardened into moralism may be better placed than some of their elders to receive surprising disclosures of what God is like. What would one expect the Lord to do about Jacob? People who believe keenly in the wrath of God may feel that it is time for Jacob to be punished for his mean trickery. People who believe that the heavenly Father must be kind, because Jesus said so, may expect God to forgive Jacob, pat him on the head, and say, 'Never mind: whatever you do I am still on your side.' Or would God lecture Jacob for not behaving better and then bless him some more, but only on conditions?

What God does is come in the form of a stranger, and wrestle with Jacob until the breaking of the day.[20] God does not overpower Jacob with anger, or comfort him with kindness, but fights with him like an equal. In this wrestling match God does not arrange who shall win, but makes Jacob struggle, with no cheating, for the blessing he wants so badly. Jacob does not get off scot-free. 'When the man saw that he did not prevail against Jacob, he touched the hollow of his thigh,' putting it out of joint. At last Jacob says, 'I will not let you go, unless you bless me.' The stranger blesses him and gives him his new name, Israel, and Jacob knows that he has seen God face to face, and yet his life is preserved. 'The sun rose upon him as he passed Penuel, limping because of his thigh.'

This story of how God came to an unlikely person at an unlikely moment in an unlikely way may disturb serene piety, but for people who find serene piety difficult it is strangely sustaining; especially as it is not a sort of erratic block, but is all of a piece with the persistent unexpectedness of God's dealings with human beings. Abraham is too old to have children, but becomes the father of a great nation.[21] Moses is diffident and is chosen to bring God's people out of Egypt.[22] David is only a shepherd boy but vanquishes Goliath[23] and becomes the Lord's Anointed.[24] The children of Israel, who know they are God's favourites, have to be told that the Day of the Lord is darkness and not light.[25] They go into exile but they find that God can be present in a strange land.[26] Job discovers that good people may suffer and that short cuts are no answer. Jonah has to be taught that even a prophet does not have God under control.

The Christian part of the story continues this paradoxical complexity. The new Covenant is like the old, indeed more so. At every stage what God does is unexpected. The Saviour is born in humble circumstances, does mighty works, teaches with authority, breaks the Sabbath, and turns upside down natural human notions of piety and of power. The people he seems to approve are generally insignificant[27] and often alien[28] or even disreputable,[29] not well-behaved, well-organized or even devout. He chooses all kinds of unreliable undesirables to be his followers and indeed they let him down.[30] He dies an accursed death; and rises again on the third day. This man who was humanly a failure is hailed as the fulfilment of ancient prophecy, recognized as present with his followers to this day and worshipped as God by monotheists.

The God who welcomes

The theme of the welcome guest is even more deeply rooted in our tradition than the theme of surprise. For human beings, as far back as history goes, hospitality is much more than an agreeable extra: it is a sacred and happy duty. The two themes of welcome and surprise meet in the perennial favourite story of the stranger who is royally received and turns out to be royal indeed. There are many tales which tell how 'some have entertained angels unawares'.[31] Philemon and Baucis welcomed Hermes and Zeus to their humble cottage. The Lord appeared to Abraham in the form of three men 'by the oaks of Mamre, as he sat at the door of his tent in the heat of the day.'[32] By contrast, the sin of Sodom, for which the city is destroyed, is a dreadful failure of hospitality.[33]

The privilege of hospitality is satisfyingly two-way. Who does the giving and who the receiving? Hosts and guests honour one another. When Abraham sees three strangers approaching, his instant reaction is to bow down before them and beg them not to pass by. 'Let a little water be brought, and wash your feet, and rest yourselves under the tree, while I fetch a morsel of bread, that you may refresh yourselves.'[34]

Because ancient Israel had a lively understanding of human hospitality as important in itself, the image of the generous human host could be a fit image for the welcoming grace of God. 'Blessed is the man, whom thou choosest . . . he shall dwell in thy court, and shall be satisfied with the pleasures of thy house, even of thy holy temple.'[35]

In the New Testament the theme of earthly and heavenly welcome keeps recurring. Hospitality is the basis of many of the parables;[36] the story of the miracle at Cana[37] would make little sense without it; St Paul attaches great importance to it.[38] In particular, the picture of Jesus as host, taking bread, blessing and giving it, runs through the stories of the feeding of the multitudes,[39] the Last Supper,[40] the supper at Emmaus[41] and the breakfast by the lakeside.[42]

The two themes of welcome and surprise are combined in the teaching of Jesus about God's welcome for people who make no claims for themselves. The unexpectedness of Jesus Christ is manifold: one conspicuous feature of his unexpectedness was the people he welcomed in God's name. The Lord Jesus made a point of encouraging thoroughly unsatisfactory characters: and not only by healing their diseases, forgiving their sins and teaching them about the kingdom, but, more remarkably, by accepting the hospitality they wanted to offer him.[43]

This was so surprising that his followers have not fully absorbed the idea yet. Christians tell one another that the Lord went about doing good, but they often fail to notice that he allowed people to do good to him, that people who were far from pious crowded around him wanting his company, that one of his favourite images for the kingdom was a party.[44] Indeed he consecrated the two-way character of hospitality.

The idea that 'all are welcome' can be caricatured as permissive: but this teaching can turn out to be more demanding in the end. When admission has conditions attached to it you know where you are. You pay the proper price, you duly receive your ticket and you walk in; or you go away, thinking how unwelcoming they are inside. An unconditional invitation seems more daunting. Accepting undeserved grace is rather like going through an alarmingly small door into an alarmingly large room. You need to bend down to get in and you are not sure what you may find on the other side.

One meaning of having faith is being willing to consider yourself included in the divine invitation. George Herbert describes himself drawing back from Love's welcome, 'Guilty of dust and sin.' He wants to go away; he offers to serve at table; but his host brushes aside his protests:

> 'You must sit down,' says Love, 'and taste my meat.'
> So I did sit and eat.[45]

Love's welcome, in a way, is 'unconditional': but above all it is unfettered. George Herbert's poem is a fine corrective to the strange tendency of good people to represent their God as mean and stingy, quite different from the Father of Jesus Christ. If there is one lesson which comes through more strongly than any other in the New Testament, it is the generosity of God. God is not going to allow human beings to refuse one another admission to the heavenly feast.

Presence of God

'Love bade me welcome' is about what God is like, not about how to get in touch with God. George Herbert was not providing data for students of religious knowledge. If he were asked the twentieth-century question, 'How do you know there is a heavenly feast at all?' he would surely not have replied, 'I have had a mystical experience of Love talking to me.' He might have talked, like a true Anglican, about scripture, tradition and reason.

Christians who nourish their faith upon the Bible can pick out the recurrent theme of God's welcome. They find that this message is confirmed by Jesus Christ. They can build upon the conviction that this is indeed what God is like, because they find that the whole structure holds up securely once the keystone has been lowered into place.[46] What they believe about the life, death and resurrection of Jesus gives Christians enough to go on. If their own spiritual lives yield only glimpses and clues, they need not feel that their faith in the generosity of God is inadequately grounded.[47]

People for whom it is hard to get in touch with God do not have to add on an extra problem of how to get in touch with Jesus. We must be careful how we talk about meeting Jesus today, because if we rush at it we shall create difficulties and invite doubt, and also miss the point.

The question is what assurance Christians can offer to the many people young and old who lack a clear awareness of God's presence. There are two answers, or rather, one answer in two parts. First, there is no need to be too sure about what they think God is doing now, if they can point to God's definitive coming in Christ. This answer requires that Jesus was a real man who could be met in a particular time and place.

That time and place were long ago. Are we getting more and more out of touch with our link to God as the years and centuries go by? Will the line snap if it is stretched out through two thousand years? The second part of the answer must be about whether Jesus Christ is still present with us; but moving on to this second step has to depend on getting the first step firm.

Christian faith is about God present then, before it can lead into beliefs about Christ present now. 'God was in Christ' means that the Creator was able and willing to be findable in one particular human life. In the Epistle to the Hebrews Jesus is described as the 'express image' of God,[48] or in newer translations the 'exact imprint'[49] or the 'stamp'[50] of 'God's very being'.

The human longing for a visible and tangible God is deep-seated but dangerous. The ban on man-made images goes far back. God's people learnt what God is like precisely by being forbidden to make likenesses of the Lord. The most vivid representation of the holiness of God was the shrine without an idol, the empty Holy of Holies.[51]

For Christians, the ban on making likenesses of God is not the whole story. The idea that humanity is meant to be an image of God goes far back too.[52] Christians believe that Jesus Christ fulfils what humankind is meant to be. This man is fit to be the definitive representation of God. We can picture God now as Jesus. Painters and sculptors have been set free to enrich the faith of Christians by providing them with images, not idols, of the Lord.

Presence of Christ

It does not follow that we can put ourselves into the picture. There is a pleasing little computer-based present for a twentieth-century child, a real printed book which tells a happy adventure story with the name of the chosen recipient inserted as the protagonist. Some Christians seem to encourage one another to read the Gospels in this way, inserting themselves into the story and picturing themselves listening to Christ talking, attending to his mighty works and following him along the dusty roads where no bicycle or car has yet been seen.

Christians who try to teach their children to have conversations with Jesus should remember that after all we cannot meet him like a contemporary. The Risen Lord is not still walking about on earth. He has 'ascended into heaven'. People today find the ascension difficult, because they are nervous of the 'three storey universe' it seems to imply. They could set aside the famous paintings and look at the Gospels,[53] which say that Jesus blessed his disciples and said goodbye to them, when he had made sure they understood that he had truly risen from the dead. The first chapter of the Acts of the Apostles adds that 'he was lifted up, and a cloud took him out of their sight'.[54] Even here there is no divine space travel but a symbolic departure, minimally miraculous if we care to interpret it so. The literal meaning of the symbolism is that the presence of Christ on earth is no longer localized in the old way. Since we cannot go on a pilgrimage to first-century Galilee, this is good news not bad.

If the departure of Jesus were the end of his story, we could hardly be Christians today. The statement in the creeds that he ascended into heaven is not about how the disciples lost sight of Jesus, but about how he is to be found. 'He who ascended is he who also ascended far above all heavens, that he might fill all things.'[55] The doctrine of the ascension is about how the same Jesus Christ who lived, died and rose became available to humanity at large by ceasing to be immediately present to a few. To start to say this kind of thing is to start to treat Jesus as more than a particularly holy man.

Just by thinking of Jesus as the risen and ascended Lord, we have got beyond the face-to-face picture. It makes sense to say that Jesus Christ is available to everyone to this day only if he is more than Jesus of Nazareth. Talking to him now is praying. It would be a mistake to begin all over again with the idea that prayer can be just like a conversation after all, once we know that Jesus is sitting at the right hand of God.

The trouble with over-simplifications is that though they are meant to be doorways they turn out to be barriers. The conversational over-simplification suggests to believers, young and old, that being a real Christian is just like being one of the apostles, except that now we know that the proper thing to do is not argue but kneel down and worship this man in middle-eastern clothes with a beard and a kind expression. The availability of Jesus now is different from his availability then.

15

Finding God in People

Christ in you, the hope of glory.

Col. 1.27

Christ in people

If we can put the picture-book idea of discipleship on one side, we may notice that already in the Gospels that version of what it means to be a disciple is not the whole story. Even in the days when Jesus walked in Galilee and called people to leave what they were doing and come with him, he did not demand or even encourage total concentration upon himself. Characteristically he pointed away from himself, to the Father and to other people.[1] We ought not to use the great metaphors which express what he has meant to his followers to reinforce the picture that our only hope is to meet him face to face. He is the doorkeeper, indeed the door.[2] He is the way, the truth and the life.[3] But however strongly Christians maintain that to find Jesus Christ is to find the way into the kingdom, Jesus himself seems to have shown a reserve sometimes amounting to anonymity.

The huge claim of his uniqueness keeps cropping up, but where the claim is most telling it emerges out of a sort of christological humility. He preaches the kingdom of God and heals sick people, and the question of his authority arises insistently out of what he says and does.[4] The distinctive humility of Jesus is not the self-abasing kind which people sometimes call 'Christ-like', but an authoritative dignity which can afford not to keep demanding recognition. This Lord directs attention towards other people as the best way of attracting his attention. Inasmuch as we take heed of one another, welcome one another, cherish one another, we take heed of him.[5] The conviction that taking heed of him is taking heed of our ultimate judge and king is fundamental but unobtrusive.

If we want to know what the presence of Christ might mean now, the teaching of Jesus about attending to one another makes an elementary and unmystical introduction. To welcome other people, including little ones, awkward ones, unpromising ones, in Christ's name is a way of looking for Christ's presence and maybe finding it. With a little care, theology, ethics and common sense, in other words, thinking, doing, and being realistic, can meet constructively here.

Christians are used to the idea that Jesus is Lord: that is doctrine. They are used to the idea that Jesus tells us to love one another: that is Christian morality. They may keep these ideas in separate compartments and not notice how the teaching about how to live and the theology are packed up together.

If we know anything about the words of Jesus, we know that his priority was God the Father. If Christians are to pay any more than lip service to this teaching, they are absolutely obliged to treat other people as God's children,[6] from nearest and dearest to neighbours and even to strangers. Children of God are not to be neglected, patronized, deceived or stereotyped, let alone bullied or cheated. They are to be cherished, appreciated, treated with courtesy, forgiven, told the truth and encouraged. If they appear simply hateful, they are to be grieved for, not gloated over. All this is more than a vague ideal. It is a demanding but elementary lesson in what it means to follow Christ. The lesson is simple enough for children. 'God loves that odd, or tiresome, or bossy, or boring person too' is surely within the comprehension of any child who has begun to understand what kindness means.

This teaching puts what we ought to do in touch with what we can do. Common sense has not much idea of how to begin to love people we do not love already, but common sense knows quite well what it is like to start off favourably disposed to someone for somebody else's sake. 'You have something in common: you are children of God' can build Christians up, when 'It is your duty to love your neighbour' casts them down.

'Human beings are God's beloved children' says something definite about God. 'This is what God is like: therefore, this is the way to live.' What we are to believe and how we are to behave belong together. It is a jump but not a big jump to go on, 'If you want to find God, this is where you can make a start.' God's children are God's representatives: we might say, God's ambassadors. God takes personally the way they are treated. Attending to one another is a way of getting in touch with God.

Christians who take the 'inasmuch' parable to heart have made one more move. They have identified Jesus as the Lord we find in one another. Other people are ikons, holy images, of Christ, who is himself the image of God. We have somewhere to look for God's presence, although Jesus is no longer walking about among us. Indirect communication can be real, and one day we shall see distinctly what has been going on all the time.

It is rash to use sayings of Christ as proof-texts, and indeed the 'inasmuch' parable does not stand unsupported. As a matter of history, St Paul became a Christian when he came to see that in persecuting Christ's followers he was persecuting Christ.[7] It would be much more rash to ignore the lesson that to reject one another is indeed to reject the Lord, and incurs the risk of being at last rejected by the Lord.[8] The prospect of a heavenly surprise, welcome or unwelcome, is serious, not just a fairy tale. So we can take the promise seriously as well as the threat,[9] and believe that all our dealings with one another will turn out to have heavenly significance.

Several corollaries follow. First, this could go patronizingly wrong. People want to be attended to for their own sakes, not for the sake of a religious reward: and that after all is the point. It is the neighbourly Samaritan who does what needs doing, while the pious priest and Levite pass by.[10] The people commended in the 'inasmuch' parable simply did not know that they were ministering to the Lord. There is no surprise if the parcel is opened too soon.

The second corollary is therefore that the privilege of representing Christ cannot be reserved for his followers. 'Christ plays in ten thousand places,' said Gerard Manley Hopkins, 'lovely in limbs, and lovely in eyes not his.'[11] The members of the Christian church have indeed the great honour of representing Christ to one another,[12] but they cannot keep Christ all to themselves. It would be seemly if Christians were quicker to grasp the idea that their God who was born as a baby and lived as a carpenter is quite likely to turn up unexpectedly, hidden in the lives of surprising people. The God who was willing even to be a foetus and to become a corpse cannot be shut up in a sanctuary. The Creator is free to range the whole creation, and there is no need to be afraid that the glory of God will somehow be spread too thin.

Christians who were less possessively anxious about serving God might have an enhanced respect for a good deal of ordinary human kindness, and fret less about other people's motivation. Can regular churchgoers imagine that an 'uncommitted' teenager who has come along just to please his parents may one day say, 'Lord, when did I think you would be disappointed and try to cheer you up?' Will it dawn upon his parents, who would most like to be convinced that their child is acceptable, that they themselves might be counted among 'the least of these' whom the Lord chooses as worth pleasing?[13]

So there is a third corollary to the belief that human beings can be representatives of Christ. If Christ is to be found in other people, it must follow that other people may find Christ in oneself: not perhaps when one tries to be like Jesus by doing them good, but when they please him by being good to us.[14] Prickly refusal to receive kindness is a disqualification from the honour of making Christ findable.

Christ in us

If other people may find Christ in us, could we ourselves directly find Christ's presence within ourselves? Many Christians have been sure that the answer to this question is Yes. The hymn known as St Patrick's Breastplate has a wide appeal:

> Christ with me, Christ before me, Christ behind me,
> Christ in me, Christ beneath me, Christ above me,
> Christ when I lie down, Christ when I sit, Christ when I arise,
> Christ in the heart of every man who thinks of me,
> Christ in the mouth of everyone who speaks of me,
> Christ in every eye that sees me,
> Christ in every ear that hears me.[15]

It is no wonder that this ancient poem is a favourite. What is more surprising is how little this way of thinking seems to shape Christian communication. This strand in Christian faith is not exactly neglected; but somehow it is hard to find out what it truly signifies. Do people often try to explain affirmations like this to their children? How do they set about relating these statements to ordinary life? To repeat them without bothering to make them one's own would be a dangerous kind of theological free-wheeling. It is odd how little puzzled Christians sometimes seem to be by the strange assertions they find themselves making.[16] God will surely forgive their confusions, but God is not going to accept parrot-talk as baby-talk.

When it is time to try to speak about the continuing presence of Jesus, the journey from the commonsensical to the mysterious needs to be taken by stages. Honesty means starting where we really are, and where we are is surely not as far on as the great saints have been. If we hope to follow their lead, the first step is to recognize that their characteristic insights are a good way ahead.

All the same, there is no need to take up a position in a dead end. Christians who neither are nor want to be mystics assume too easily that just because Jesus is Lord they can settle for over-simplified ideas about knowing God. They imagine encountering Jesus Christ today and having reverent conversations. So they get stuck in the discouraging picture-book piety.[17] It is more realistic, and also more promising, to acknowledge first that for most of us God is still looking over our shoulders, whispering in our ears, sending us messages, showing us things, not confronting us directly.[18] This is not defeatism but a good place to start.

Belief that Jesus was God-made-man means that all this is better grounded, not that it is superseded. Jesus Christ offers an answer to the objection that we are making up our own faith. Christians have a refreshed belief in the possibility of God's presence, not an extra divine personage to look out for.

The next step is to try to enter into more of our heritage. Religious people have always believed that even when we cannot find God, God has no difficulty in finding us. God is supposed to be closer to us than any human being can be:

For the word of God is living and active, sharper than any two-edged sword, piercing to the division of soul and spirit, of joints and marrow, and discerning the thoughts and intentions of the heart. And before him no creature is hidden, but all are open and laid bare to the eyes of him with whom we have to do.[19]

The odd thing about this evocative passage from the Epistle to the Hebrews is that though mysterious it is not controversial. It picks up ideas which run right through the Bible, for instance in some of the most favourite psalms:

O Lord, thou hast searched me out and known me: thou knowest my down-sitting and mine up-rising; thou understandest my thoughts long before . . .[20]

When J. A. T. Robinson in *Honest to God*[21] popularized the idea that God is the 'ground of our being', for many people he made it easier not harder to find God. When a transcendent God 'up there' seems too far away, the idea of God's presence within us, technically called God's 'immanence', can come to the rescue.

There is no escaping the fact that this curious notion of God within us is characteristic of Christianity.[22] Christians do not go in for the idea of human souls being somehow absorbed into the Absolute and losing their own existence. On the contrary, Christians talk about ways of being united to God which bring out people's own particular individuality. In other words, Christian 'immanence' has everything to do with Christian love.

Even humanly, it is a mistake to think of a person as a simple atom, absolutely separate from other atoms. The boast of the jolly miller,

I care for nobody, no not I,
And nobody cares for me

is neither characteristically human, happy nor particularly admirable; and is probably not even true. People are born, grow up, live and flourish by depending upon one another. At the best, people become themselves in union with other people. There are things we say about the ways human beings are capable of being related to one another which at least begin to get us on to the right wavelength for talking about divine indwelling.[23]

Christians add something like this, that whatever the closeness of God to every one of us means, the risen Christ shares in it. The idea that Jesus of Nazareth is 'the cosmic Christ', in whom 'all the fullness of God was pleased to dwell'[24] sounds difficult: but Christians cannot afford to ignore this way of speaking and then wonder why God seems to be absent, any more than they can afford to use these words casually and then wonder why their faith is not more catching.

The disciples of Jesus told stories about how he did things which ordinary human beings do: growing up 'in wisdom and stature',[25] learning, eating and drinking, making friends, teaching, healing, forgiving, suffering, dying. They have never stopped here. They have always filled in the plain picture with mystery. The mystery is deeply enfolded in our earliest records. There is no getting back to a version uncomplicated by theology.

The conviction that Jesus had risen touched off a sort of explosion of variegated affirmations about his mysterious continuing nearness. The 'inasmuch' parable is the tip of an iceberg. The vivid certainty of the presence of the risen Christ appears in different contexts in the New Testament, from the seemingly straightforward promise 'I am with you always'[26] at the end of Matthew, to the high doctrine that 'in him all things hold together' of the Epistle to the Colossians.[27] What has been called 'Christ-mysticism', the belief that we abide in Christ and he in us, is basic Christianity in the writings of St Paul[28] and in the Fourth Gospel.[29]

'Indwelling' is a technicality; but if Christians shy away from the ideas it can stand for, that Christ is present around and within us, they are a long way from the faith the early Christians learnt, in the days when epistles were letters to the churches and the gospel was first written down in Gospels. We are rightly sure that our faith cannot be abstruse, beyond most of us and accessible only to the learned. It may well be mysterious, beyond all of us but resonant with significance we can enter into gradually.

When we try to teach what we believe to children, we may well hesitate to try to explain 'immanence' too soon. What matters is not to teach a faith with no space for immanence. If older Christians can sit loose to the picture of God confronting them, and put more emphasis on the idea of God beside them, they make room to bring in the idea of God within them, whenever this seems to become suitable.

St Augustine preached on God's indwelling to a presumably ordinary congregation in a sermon on the verse from Psalm 31, 'Thou shalt hide them privily by thine own presence . . .':

> It is in God's face, then, that we shall be hidden. Do you expect to hear me describe the hiding place of God's countenance? Cleanse your heart so that He Himself may enlighten you, that He whom you invoke may take possession of you. Be you His dwelling place and He will be your dwelling place: let Him abide in you and you will abide in Him. If you welcome Him into your heart during this life, He will welcome you with His face when life is ended.[30]

Christians have talked about 'indwelling' and 'abiding', not to make life difficult for the uninstructed, but because they have found that these ideas answer to their experience. If Christians today both attend to their tradition and also are honest about whatever modest experience they themselves have, they give their faith a chance to grow.

16

Finding God in Things

Raise the stone, and there thou shalt find me, cleave the wood
and there am I.

Oxyrhynchus papyri

Down to earth

If faith is to grow, faith needs to be fed. That assertion is better
taken too literally than not literally enough. Of course what it
means is spiritual growth, but 'spiritual' is a difficult word. Lay
people on the whole are chary of it. It is certainly not part of the
vocabulary of children. 'Spiritual' is apt to sound like jargon.
People who talk about 'spirituality' frighten off the others who
easily think this is not for them.

To be spiritual could be one of those important goals which
elude us when we aim at them directly. When people try to be
original they notoriously fall flat. The happiest human beings are
not the ones who search for happiness but the ones who put their
hearts into what they are doing and find happiness has crept up
on them. Likewise, the most spiritual people could be the ones
who are not much given to thinking about whether they are
spiritual or not. The way to enter eventually into the deepest
mysteries is to start where one is: as a child, an adolescent or a
grown-up, muddled, sinful, doubtful, critical, hopeful, faithful,
or a mixture of all these.

For Christians who affirm that God took human flesh, a
spiritual faith can and must be an earthly faith. 'Spiritual'
presumably means 'in touch with Spirit': and if 'in touch' is
allowed to get too far from its physical meaning it may turn out
not to have much meaning at all. Human beings are embodied
creatures. To be in touch, literally or metaphorically, we need

some way of taking hold.[1] The Word of God has somehow or other to be made flesh for people to hear it.

Christians believe that God was embodied in the life of Jesus Christ. But now we are nearly two thousand years away from that incarnation. Faith can feel quite wobbly with undernourishment. The Holy Spirit can seem like a ghost and Holy Scripture can seem like a corpse. When we want to know how to set about finding God ourselves and encouraging other people, the question 'What kind of body can God use to communicate with us?' is a good question. It has suggested variegated answers. We can indeed look hopefully for God in nature, in Christ, in the church, in the Bible, in one another, and in our own selves.

Christians can look, and will surely be challenged about what they believe they have found. They can reply that they have kept finding glimpses of a God who has a distinctive character: a God who is always beyond us, but who comes to welcome us.[2] They cannot prove, but they can invite. 'Oh taste, and see, how gracious the Lord is.'[3]

Because God is Spirit, and God's presence is spiritual presence, it may become a problem how literal this invitation can be. Are these glimpses of God too manifold and too vague to be real food for faith? If God's presence is practically everywhere, does it mean much to say so? In particular, if the Spirit of God is present especially in the human spirit, God may seem to be altogether too well hidden. Human beings too can be lovable, welcoming, even in a way worshipful: so do they convey or cover up God's lovability, God's welcome and God's worshipfulness? It is part of what it means to say that God is always beyond us, that whenever we try to say anything specific about God there is likely to come a point where somebody begins to say, 'That's all very well, but . . .'; and this somebody may well be oneself.

We easily lose our grip on spiritual presence. We may hold on to everything that has been suggested so far, but it would be good to have something still more definite and down-to-earth to offer. Christians of all people ought not to assume that the idea of physical presence must be unworthy of God. If God can nominate human beings as representatives, God can surely designate things as 'means of grace'. Though human beings look more adequate bearers of the divine presence, it could after all be easier to find God in things. If objects we can see and handle can be given meaning beyond themselves, they may be able to make God's continuing welcome today definite enough to be credible.

Carriers of meaning

The destination of this line of thought is not hard to guess, but to start talking about God's sacramental presence forthwith would still be too hasty. To many people the rite which is variously called the eucharist, the mass, holy communion, or the Lord's Supper, is a strange business. Loyal Christians have to accept the bread and wine as somehow signifying, or even actually being, the Body and Blood of Christ; but this ritual performance hardly seems a promising way for people to set about finding God's presence unless they know pretty well where they stand already. What baffles or even repels many grown-ups is not likely to be much help when they want to introduce children to the Christian faith.

For 'the sacrament' to come alive it needs to be considered first as *a* sacrament. Bread and wine have plenty of human meaning before they are used in this mysterious way. Human beings do not always treat physical objects as neutral lumps of inert stuff. We know perfectly well that material things are indeed raw material. They are capable of carrying all kinds of meaning.[4]

Bread and milk signify more or less cosy childishness; bread and water convey reprobation; whereas the popping of champagne corks mean celebration even to people who prefer still wine. A ring on one's finger symbolizes belonging. A medal for long service is worth more than the metal of which it is made. To draw down the blinds has had agonizing significance at times when people have been especially conscious of the fragility of life. Flowers say 'Thank-you' or 'I'm so sorry' or 'Many happy returns' or sometimes 'I love you', more simply than words. Cutting a cake is a complex symbol of receiving congratulations and offering hospitality. For physical creatures, physical things are ways of getting in touch. There is nothing 'materialist' in the bad sense about emphasizing that human creatures are indeed physical creatures. On the contrary, when people discover how to endow matter with meaning they are beginning to transcend materialism, not succumbing to it.

Before it can make much sense to say that God has appointed things as carriers of divine significance, we must seize hold of the idea that human beings can appoint things as carriers of human significance. Then we can start to say that the universe in which we are placed in a sacramental universe, in which the physical is not only real in its own right but is a fit vehicle for spiritual meaning. Gerard Manley Hopkins said, 'The world is charged with the grandeur of God.'[5]

As Elizabeth Barrett Browning put it, even more vigorously:

> Earth's crammed with heaven,
> And every common bush afire with God;
> But only he who sees, takes off his shoes,
> The rest sit round it and pluck blackberries.[6]

Was she being somewhat defeatist? When a day in the country is a holiday, a down-to-earth enterprise like brambling can take on a sort of magical glory akin to holiness. Eating newly-picked berries is more festive than taking them home and making them into a pudding. It is not such a long step to the recognition of God's glory in God's creatures. Particular sacraments are a way of focussing that recognition.

The word 'sacrament' sounds difficult but the idea it stands for is well within children's grasp. To begin to understand that things carry meaning there is no need to be mature, only to be human. Three-year-olds thoroughly appreciate ritual: the birthday candles to be blown out, the musical box only Granny is allowed to wind up, the arrangements of Teddies at bedtime, the story full of repetitions which must not be abbreviated. The careful performance of such a rite is an outward and visible sign of an inward and surely not unspiritual human grace.[7]

The sacraments which are the outward and visible signs of divine grace do not belong to a separate world from these human realities. The use of set forms has nothing to do with legalism. We *do this* in the proper way, not to force anything upon other people but to find a promised blessing. God may be found in countryside or town, in a bramble bush or a tube train, but surely it makes sense to go where our tradition tells us God has undertaken to be present.[8]

Real presence

'Real presence', to Protestant-minded Christians, has a Romish sound to it, because the presence of Christ in the sacrament is easily confused with transubstantiation, and transubstantiation is more easily caricatured than explained. Christians have sometimes thought that there are simply two alternatives: *either* the bread and wine undergo an invisible metaphysical change into Christ's flesh and blood: *or* they remain only bread and wine, Christ is not really there at all, and the sacrament is no more than a memorial service at which we gratefully remember that he died for us.

Protestant and Catholic Christians may distinguish 'real presence' from 'transubstantiation'. If Christ is present, really present, in this sacrament, it does not automatically follow that the bread and wine are miraculously though imperceptibly changed. Some of us think that 'transubstantiation' is a way of speaking which depends upon a particular philosophy and is better left on one side when that philosophy is not ours.

Others believe that transubstantiation must still be illuminating and indeed needful for our souls' health, and that they can and should try to explain it. If they feel bound by this loyalty, they ought at least to be aware of the dangers. It needs to be said that transubstantiation is a difficult doctrine commonly mistaken for an easy one, which has formed people's notions of what this sacrament is supposed to mean in ways which have been more trouble than help.

Of course people have treasured the belief that the bread and wine actually become Christ's Body and Blood. They feel most vividly assured that the Lord really is there.[9] No wonder anything less miraculous seems second best. Catholics feel encouraged and Protestants vaguely defensive. Christians of all kinds find it hard to extricate themselves from a time-honoured caricature of what this rite means, with overtones of cannibalism which nobody wants to face.

Sensitive people have been worried by the idea that in the sacrifice of the mass faithful Christians kill their God and feed upon his dead body. According to the story of the Mass of Bolsena, immortalized by Raphael, in 1263 a priest's doubts about the miracle of transubstantiation were resolved by what one might call a secondary miracle, when blood issued from the host at the moment of consecration. May one think that when he doubted his state was the more gracious? It is understandable that where the doctrine of transubstantiation has prevailed 'non-communicating attendance' at the eucharist has also prevailed. Devout people may be happier adoring than eating.

All this seems a long way from the Lord sharing bread and wine with his friends: yet Catholic Christians have a right to point out that the eucharist is more than the Lord's Supper: it cannot be detached from the sacrifice of the cross. The ideas which transubstantiation seems to overstate certainly take their rise from the New Testament.[10] As P. J. Fitzpatrick puts it, our tradition is *both revered and unsatisfactory*:[11] a situation in which 'embarrassment is profitable'.[12]

It is not surprising when people are in no hurry to encourage their children to become communicants. Surely the eucharist is too difficult for children, when it seems too difficult for grown-ups? To try to understand what holy communion means can surely wait until they are older? But by the time they are old enough they may have given up any lively hope of finding God's presence.

There is a roundabout route which is not too arduous, which leads right away from the two unhappy alternatives, only-too-physical presence or practical absence. Before embarking upon this route we need a glimpse of where it leads. Metaphysical arguments about what happens to the bread and wine are a false start. The best hope of finding the real presence of the Lord is to begin with the question how God can get in touch with embodied creatures.[13]

At the Last Supper Jesus was alive not dead. When he gave the bread and wine to signify in some way his body and blood his heart was beating and his blood was circulating. Nobody was going to eat his dead body. If transubstantiation gives people that idea, then they are better without it. What nourishes Christians is the *life* of Christ. Whatever we say will be an over-simplification, but we can head towards the idea that real presence has to do with indwelling. Then we can go on to relate all this to his death.[14]

Nourishment

It is not for nothing that the imagery of the heavenly feast is so prevalent in our tradition.[15] Human beings, like all the other animals, need nourishment to stay alive. Deprived of food, we starve. Short of food, we lose energy for thought as well as for action. Brains, eyes and ears need feeding as well as muscles. It would be strange if God the Creator were unconcerned with the needs of physical creatures.

It is a short and easy step, well within the capacity of children, to the idea that for human beings food and drink mean more than physical wellbeing. A good diet builds up bodies: and also we can say that eating and drinking, and the way we eat and drink, build up spirits. People who are working hard need to stop and have a meal, not only because they will run out of energy and even collapse sooner or later, but as a sign that life is more than work. People are not made to go on and on without a break. They get hungry for something to chew upon with their mouths, and they also get hungry for a change and a rest and something else to think about: something, as it were, to chew upon with their minds and hearts.

Meals, formal, informal, or even solitary, are mini-holidays. 'Refreshment' has strong metaphorical as well as physical meaning. Time, place and company are part of the refreshment, not extra to it.

A human being is not the kind of animal which generally fends for itself. Much more often, from babyhood to maturity, people feed one another and are fed. Even lone occupants of bed-sitters can buy convenience foods which have been prepared by other people for them to live on. To be the one who cooks for the others has its powerful satisfactions. To offer people food is one of the plainest ways of doing something definite for them. 'Just a cup of tea and a biscuit' which tells a guest 'I'm glad to see you' has become something of a cliché, simply because what it stands for has such deep human significance.

Eating together signifies interdependence, trust and welcome. There is nothing sophisticated about the sharing of food. Hospitality is fundamentally, indeed primitively, human. To eat somebody's salt creates a sacred bond. Macbeth's horror at his intended treachery to Duncan, his guest, is as strong as his horror at betraying Duncan his king.[16] The word 'companion' by derivation is someone with whom one eats bread.[17]

Meals can 'express bodily processes of understanding and communicating that accompany and may even transcend words'.[18] This is the kind of context in which Abraham hastened to provide cakes and 'curds, and milk, and the calf that he had prepared' to set before the three strangers; 'and he stood by them under the tree while they ate'.[19]

Sacrifices

This is also the context for primitive sacrifice. In earliest times people who chose an animal out of their flocks especially for God may have imagined themselves as cooking God's dinner. If they had the housewifely thought that God owed them gratitude for what they had taken all this trouble to prepare, they invited rebuke.

> If I be hungry, I will not tell thee: for the whole world is mine, and all that is therein.
> Thinkest thou that I will eat bulls' flesh: and drink the blood of goats?[20]

It is easy enough to patronize them for their naivety, or even to blame them anachronistically for their brutality. But the more one likes to side morally with prophet and psalmist, the less one can afford to outgrow the conviction that everything belongs to God and ought to be offered to God.

Nor is it at all needful to outgrow the idea of eating and drinking with God. To ask the Creator to be present at human meals to bless the produce of the earth for us is an even more basic notion than sacrifice.[21] Grown-up people and children alike do well to imagine God as somebody who is always pleased to be asked to join in: a God who accepts invitations.[22] What the psalmist was criticizing was not a picture of God sniffing the dinner cooking in happy anticipation, but a picture of God depending on what human beings could be bothered to provide. 'For all the beasts of the forest are mine: and so are the cattle upon a thousand hills.'[23]

It is another short step for Christians to move on to their particular example of the Lord who accepted invitations. If Jesus Christ represented God, the picture of Jesus in the Gospels fills in and backs up the picture of a God who is willing to join in. The God Jesus reveals is not averse to the material world in which human creatures live.

17

The Breaking of Bread

I realized that I was far away from thee in the land of
unlikeness, as if I heard thy voice from on high: 'I am the food of
strong men; grow and you shall feed on me; nor shall you
change me, like the food of your flesh into yourself, but you
shall be changed into my likeness.'

St Augustine, *Confessions* VII 11

Table companions

Whatever we know or do not know about the Lord Jesus, we
know that he could be hungry and thirsty.[1] It is evident that he
enjoyed food and drink.[2] An ascetic might be surprised and even
a little shocked at the importance of meals in the Gospel stories.
When Jairus' daughter is healed the first thing she needs is
something to eat.[3] Peter's mother-in-law is able to get up and
look after them as soon as her fever has gone down.[4] Sometimes
there is so much coming and going that there is hardly time to
eat.[5]

Jesus and his disciples ate many ordinary meals together. The
stories about special occasions arise out of the everyday eating
and drinking which is taken for granted. Much of his teaching is
given as 'table talk'. If we believe that Jesus showed what God is
like in his way of living as well as in his dying, it matters that his
welcoming hospitality and his readiness to be a guest[6] were
thoroughly down to earth: not 'spiritual' in the way we generally
use the word.

A special occasion described in all four Gospels is the feeding of
a great crowd who had followed Jesus out into the wilds and
found themselves stranded without provisions.[7] The Evangelists
are confident that what Jesus did for them was a miracle. Some

people who find miracles worrying prefer to point out what can be done when somebody sets a good example by sharing. While traditionalists and liberals take up their stances, they may miss what Jesus plainly did:

> Taking the five loaves and the two fish he looked up to heaven, and blessed, and broke the loaves, and gave them to his disciples to set before the people; and he divided the two fish among them all.[8]

Before the meal began Jesus took the food into his hands, gave thanks, broke the bread and gave it to everybody who was there. Probably he used the familiar words he and his disciples would have been taught from childhood: 'Blessed be Thou, O Lord our God, King of the universe, who bringest forth bread from the earth.' This little Jewish ritual was part of their lives.[9]

The special occasion in the wilderness was one of many times when Jesus took bread and blessed it. There came a day when he did this in the consciousness that he was about to be arrested and killed. The earliest account we have[10] of the Last Supper tells how

> the Lord Jesus on the night when he was betrayed took bread, and when he had given thanks, he broke it, and said, 'This is my body which is for you. Do this in remembrance of me.'

There have been many arguments about what he said and what he meant. It makes a good start to bear in mind that what we call the 'institution of the sacrament' was rooted in the everyday ritual of breaking bread together. It is easier to understand what it means to *do this* in his name by asking first what was the same about the Last Supper, before asking what was different.

When Jesus said that the bread somehow represented his body he was laying meaning upon meaning. 'Eucharist' means 'thanksgiving', and before the sacrament is anything else it is thanksgiving for nourishment. Nourishment is a material notion, and more. Physical bread and wine are already full of meaning: 'wind that maketh glad the heart of man ... and bread to strengthen man's heart'.[11] People who eat and drink together endow physical sustenance with more than physical meaning.

Nourishment becomes companionship. Whenever Jesus took bread and blessed it he was consecrating a kind of sacrament.

The difference this time was that the companionship was under the imminent shadow of the cross. The presence of Jesus, which Christians believe with hindsight was the real presence of God, was to be violently removed from them. Could he be present to them any more, and if so what assurance could he give them? The meaning he added to the bread and wine at the Last Supper has been taken by his followers ever since as a promise of continuing presence. Since the eucharist belongs in this context, there is no need to think of it as either a difficult and gloomy mystery, or a merely social occasion. To break this bread and drink this cup means the continuation of companionship: not just any companionship, but companionship with the Lord who died and was raised from death.

Presence renewed

What right do Christians have to believe that they may claim this promise and find the Lord's real presence by *doing this* in his name? Nobody can be literally present just by saying, 'Count me in' or 'I'll be with you in spirit.' As Jesus was so soon to be physically absent, what do we mean by saying that he is there, when in the plainest sense he is not?

Any of us can hold a departed friend in remembrance. A memorial service may be a comfort. People take a lot of trouble to do it 'just as he would have wished', feeling that this is something they can still do for him. When those who are left behind carry on doing all the ordinary things they used to do together, memories may become especially vivid, and they say 'we felt he was there with us'. They particularly cherish his belongings he has now bequeathed to them, which seem to be endowed with a sort of sacramental quality. If they believe in heaven they may feel sure of meeting again one day. These ways of remembering are comforts, sometimes powerful comforts, for present absence. But there is more to the eucharist than a loving memorial. The word translated 'remembrance'[12] has overtones of 're-calling'.

Meaning has to be based upon reality. The old companionship was rooted in physical facts. They literally ate and drank together, and were nourished. If the eucharist really means more than eating and drinking together and being spiritually encouraged by thinking about Jesus, it must also be grounded in some reality more than bare assertions. Austin Farrer said 'He gave them the sacrament by eating with them; he made it their salvation by his death.'[13]

At the Last Supper the bread, blessed, broken and given in the familiar way, already had human meaning beyond the merely physical. It could strengthen their hearts. The extra fact, only too real, which grounded the extra sacramental meaning was that the actual body of Jesus was about to be broken. People who find the idea of sacrifice a help will have more to say here. The basis is the belief that somehow he died for our sakes.

If the death of Jesus were all, it would be just a sad story. There would be no backing for pledges he gave before he died. Christians also believe that death could not hold him. The double reality that he went right through death and that he was triumphantly raised backs up the conviction that he spoke with authority. He had the right to designate bread and wine as carriers of his living presence.[14]

When Jesus died on the cross he was truly taken away. Traditionally the church does not celebrate the sacrament on Good Friday or Holy Saturday. But on the third day his friends, women and men, met him again, more alive than ever. Whatever exactly happened on the first Easter morning,[15] the idea comes through strongly that his body, however spiritual, was still manifested in a physical way.

According to Luke, the two disciples recognized him at Emmaus in the breaking of bread:

> When he was at table with them, he took the bread and blessed, and broke it, and gave it to them. And their eyes were opened and they recognized him; and he vanished out of their sight.[16]

In Jerusalem, the risen Christ asked the eleven, 'Have you anything here to eat?' and ate a piece of fish before their eyes to show them that he was real.[17] In Galilee, according to the postscript to the Fourth Gospel,[18] he invited them to 'Come and have breakfast': and then they 'knew it was the Lord'.

People who are nervous of being thought naive and literal-minded are tempted to spiritualize their belief. To eat grilled fish hardly seems a very holy idea. Surely the Risen Lord was Spirit? Of course: but to over-emphasize this can be a hindrance, especially when older people are tempted to treat the literal notions they have outgrown as cast-offs good enough for the young ones. The main idea, simple enough for children but not too elementary for their elders, is that Jesus was still the same person when he came back to his friends.

Keeping in touch

If we believe that he is still the same person, now that he has 'ascended into heaven',[19] the belief that he 'lives today in bread and wine'[20] is thoroughly congruous with the rest of what we believe about him. That he gave us physical ways of keeping *in touch* fits perfectly with what we know about his life on earth.

We can go further back, into the history of God's people. We may say that it is characteristic of God the Creator to give human beings material means of keeping in touch. Though the children of Israel were not allowed graven images, they could offer God their produce and invite God to partake of their meals.[21] Christians who look for the real presence of the Lord in bread and wine are in that tradition. They believe they are accepting the invitation of Jesus Christ, who died and rose, to eat and drink with him. They are part of the same company as the earliest Christians who 'devoted themselves to the apostles' teaching and fellowship, to the breaking of bread and prayers';[22] and with all the others down the centuries who have *done this*. The earliest known picture of the eucharist is a third century painting in Rome, in the Catacomb of S. Priscilla, of seven people sitting at a table. They are our fellow Christians doing what the church still does.[23]

This sacrament has many names and many meanings. 'The breaking of bread' is the simplest. The eucharist, the thanks-giving, is accurate and ecumenical. Other names, the holy communion, the mass, the Lord's Supper, have been used by separated Christians and can seem partisan. There is no need to exclude other people's names or other people's meanings.

Ways of understanding this sacrament have ranged from the poetic inspiration of George Herbert's 'The Agonie',

> Love is that liquor sweet and most divine,
> Which my God feels as bloud, but I as wine

to the trustful agnosticism, not to be confused with cynicism, of the verse ascribed to Queen Elizabeth I,

> His was the word that spake it,
> He took the bread and brake it,
> And what his word did make it,
> I do believe and take it.

There is the historical enthusiasm of Dom Gregory Dix, 'Was ever another command so obeyed?';[24] and the sturdy legalism of Shakespeare's Thomas Mowbray, Duke of Norfolk, in his quarrel with Bolingbroke:

> But ere I last received the sacrament
> I did confess it, and exactly begg'd
> Your Grace's pardon, and I hope I had it.[25]

It would be a pity to forget the theological balance of Daniel Brevint, the seventeeth-century Puritan divine who in his youth was rector of the parish of Grouville in Jersey, and who later was a Doctor of Divinity at Oxford and Dean of Lincoln:

> At the holy table the people meet to worship God, and God is present to meet and bless his people. Here we are in a special manner invited to offer up to God our souls, our bodies, and whatever we can *give* and God offers to us the body and blood of his Son, and all the other blessings which we need to *receive* . . .[26]

'The devil', he said,[27] 'has been so busy about this Sacrament, driving men either to make it a *false god*, or an *empty ceremony*'; but what Brevint found was sustenance: 'Lo, he is become to me the bread of life. Let us go, then, to take and eat it.'[28]

Take this

The eucharist is not the only way to get in touch with God, nor the whole of the Christian life. Sacraments are means of grace, not 'proper channels' by which God has to be approached. They are there to help, not to make people who find them no help feel like inadequate outsiders. There are ways of giving priority to the eucharist which make worshippers into an in-group. Even the friendly invitation, 'Let all who love the Lord draw near' can seem to dismiss out of hand the different reasons people may have for feeling unable to draw near.

Loyal Christians need to take hold of the unfamiliar idea that this rite which matters so much is available but not compulsory.[29] Oddly enough, the more the eucharist is built up as all-important, the less accessible it appears. Of course it is paradoxical to say that we could possibly over-rate the promised presence of God in our midst; but there are ways of being possessive about God's presence which start to slip into idolatry. There is an easy slide from the compulsory to the compulsive.

The test is whether in their ritual acts people are looking out for the living God, always several steps ahead, who condescends to be here but who may turn up anywhere; or whether they think that to *do this* in the correct way is in its own right the quintessence of Christian living. If the sacrament is isolated in church, wrapped in specialized piety, it may even be a stumbling-block to people outside who are wondering where they might find a God to worship. But the sacrament does not have to be isolated in church, any more than the Last Supper was isolated from all the other meals when Jesus broke bread. Almost anything in God's creation can be a sign of God's presence. When Teilhard de Chardin[30] found himself stranded in the steppes, with 'neither bread, nor wine, nor altar', instead of complaining that he had no way of keeping in touch he proceeded to make the whole earth his altar and offer to God 'all the labours and sufferings of the world'.

The eucharist is special because it is a given sign. It is meant to be a doorway, not a hurdle to be jumped.[31] It is a way of keeping in touch, because it connects what Christ used to do on earth with what his followers continue to do in his name and with everyday nourishment and company.

Surely it is time for some fresh thinking about welcoming new Christians. Are children too young to receive this nourishment in company with their elders? If we imagine that they must wait until they are 'old enough to understand', how many of us ought to be communicants at all? In the Eastern Orthodox churches babies receive communion. In the Church of Rome First Communion is given at a younger age than is usual among Protestants.

The idea of 'wait until you are older' belongs with the idea that the Lord's Supper is too holy to be celebrated frequently at all. There is a long-standing and honourable Protestant tradition, in which many good Christians have lived their lives, of non-eucharistic Sunday worship for everyone. Now that in many churches the parish communion has taken over, the bread and wine are still not for the children. Anyone who is not confirmed may be invited to come up for 'a blessing'. Indeed this policy is welcoming and often gives pleasure, but there is a question mark against it none the less. In the long run, when the message for children is 'You can't have this, only that', several misleading messages are likely to get through: the people the Lord treated as most important seem to be devalued, the powerful symbol of the laying on of hands is made ordinary, and God's blessing itself becomes a second best.

When blessing is offered instead of a sacrament, how can young Christians come to understand that a sacrament is indeed the way blessing is conveyed? There are many conflicting considerations which ought to be given due weight, but at least it can be said that reverence and hopeful expectation seem less difficult for many children than for some grown-ups, and one thing we want to avoid is to nip their trustfulness in the bud.

Heavenly feast

The eucharist has many meanings. One meaning is that it makes Christians part of the communion of saints. When Christians meet together to eat this bread and drink this cup they are offered a kind of foretaste of heavenly celebration. That is a lofty hope. In all honesty, few people will feel conscious of its fulfilment in their own present experience; but it can be put more modestly. When we keep in touch in this way we are latching on to the life of heaven, which is going on whether we realize it or not.

We may ask how we know that the life of heaven is real. The reasons for believing in it are the same as the reasons for believing that Christianity is true. Too often Christians have tried to specify in some detail what the next world must be like; and too many of these human ideas have been more likely to shock people of goodwill than encourage them, let alone convert them. Tourist guides to hell, purgatory and paradise may be good reading but can be misleading for planning pilgrimages. A certain amount of agnosticism, not about whether there really is another world, but about what it is like, would be more prudent and seemly.

Heaven is where God is and where human beings may hope one day to be with God. That is simple enough for children. If grown-ups say anything less than that among themselves, they are leaving out so much of our tradition that their faith is not fully Christian, even if it is the best they can do at the moment. The hints and glimpses people find of God's presence in this world are indications that heaven is real too. To back up heavenly hopes, what we need are pledges, not pictures. The most down-to-earth pledges we have are the scriptures and the sacraments.

If we can find God, we can leave our heavenly hopes in God's hands. We need to say more, if we can, about this God we believe is there to be found. When we get out of our depth, that is just what we ought to expect. There is no need for blind leaps of faith. We can paddle in the shallows and when we are ready we can plunge into the big waves.

18

God the Holy Trinity

So, the all-great, were the all-loving too –

Robert Browning[1]

Three in One

Trying to understand is not presumptuous, and not to try may be defeatist. There is a strong base to build upon. The Hebrew scriptures are the record of how God's people learnt that God is One, that God is holy, and that God's holiness is not impersonal but loving. The New Testament is the record of how God's love came down to earth in a human life. Christians enter into this double heritage. They reaffirm that God is One, and then they complicate this by announcing that God is Three: Father, Son and Spirit.

The attempt to make sense of their experience plunges Christians into paradox. There is no harm in that. If scientists find the physical universe strange, how much stranger the God who made it must be. We can say to children, 'You are not old enough to understand,' and add, 'nor are we.' We are used to the idea that biochemistry and nuclear physics are about reality though they are beyond the understanding of most of us.[2]

Mathematicians are awestruck by the beauty of their difficult equations. Christian theologians may be still more awestruck when they find themselves impelled to believe that the Creator of everything is not mathematically simple but complex. They do not deny that God is One, any more than Einstein contradicted Newton; but they have to make things difficult, to account for all the data of which they have become aware.

Human beings cannot fathom God. It is entirely in order to say, 'This is a mystery': but there is a condition. What we like to call

162

mystery must not be mystification. There must be some reason for believing that there really is something here which is beyond our understanding. This reason will generally be that we trust other people who have gone deeper. The doctrine that God is Three as well as One is a way of interpreting the experience of Christian saints. Though attempts to tidy faith up have sometimes got out of hand, the doctrine of the Trinity cannot be set aside as if it concerned only the experts. It is an attempt to answer real questions and reckon with real data.

The church has arrived at a formula, that God is Three in One. If people find this baffling, it is understandable that they simply leave it out of the faith they try to teach their children. Though baffling, this doctrine of the Holy Trinity is basic. If it is evaded, the belief that God was in Christ is lost in vagueness and inconsistency. Is it in order to worship Jesus Christ? When Jesus died, was God really there? Unless beginners are given a clue that our God is not simply One, what will come through to them will not be mystery but muddle. As soon as people begin to tell their children about Jesus, they are saying something or other about the Trinity.

The questions are not optional technicalities. Did God come? Or did the Father send his Son on this dangerous mission and watch from on high? Is the Spirit He or It, or maybe She? Did the Spirit come at Pentecost to replace Jesus, and what was the Spirit doing before that, besides moving upon the face of the waters, and appearing from time to time in the form of a dove?[3] The doctrine of the Trinity takes its rise from the Christian conviction that Father, Son and Spirit are all real but not separate; and especially from Christian experience of praying *to* the Father, *through* the Son, *in* the Holy Spirit.[4] We can be glad, not alarmed, that the New Testament does not provide one authorized theology, but offers various approaches[5] to the idea that God is Three in One.

A line of thought which has led all this way towards the doctrine of God the Holy Trinity might be expected to culminate in a blaze of inspiration, or failing that to fizzle out in despondency. On the contrary, to ground one's faith in the Trinity makes one less dependent upon blazing inspiration. We may celebrate, not apologize, when we find that there are depths in God we cannot fathom. Our inadequacy is not a negative fact about us but a positive fact about God. To say that God is Three in One is partly a way of putting into words the conviction that we cannot exhaust God's greatness. God has a life beyond our understanding. Christians still live by hints and glimpses. Showing one another things is more promising than proclaiming. Muted and diffident ways of speaking show more than ringing affirmations. Here if anywhere we may go gently and patiently, as far as we find we can.

Christians sometimes feel as if upholding the faith meant carrying God upon their shoulders; but God is responsible for the carrying. 'I have made, and I will bear; I will carry and will save.'[6] In a way, we can relax. There is no need to put ourselves or one another under 'all-or-nothing' spiritual pressure. God is surely more pleased with our modesty than our confidence. The devil is in despair, according to C. S. Lewis, when somebody sets aside attempts to fix God clearly in mind and prays, 'Not to what I think thou art but to what thou knowest thyself to be.'[7]

God is love

Must mystery be contradiction? Plenty of people are only too happy to assume that there is no need to bother with Christian doctrine because it is evidently nonsense. Instead of doggedly reiterating their Three-in-One formula, Christians who believe it is true may expect it also to apply to human life in ways they can understand. We have this difficult paradoxical doctrine, but we need not say 'Take it or leave it.' We can pick out aspects of human life which make the Three-in-Oneness of God easier to understand; and we can show why the Three-in-Oneness matters to us and is worth explaining.

We cannot talk Christian sense for long without talking about love. Mathematical paradox is allowable and even exciting, but cannot be enough. We hesitate and are shy, because words like 'love' and 'relationship' are so battered by use and misuse.[8] They are hard-worked because they are fundamental, and although they sometimes need a rest, when we are talking about what really matters we must go on working them hard.

If human beings are made in God's image, the truth about God is likely to bear some relation to the truth about human beings. If we have reason to believe that God is One but not simply One, it should be a help to remember that a human being is not simply one like an isolated atom, either.[9] People depend upon one another, and also they identify with one another. They suffer and rejoice with their friends, their spouses, their children. They give each other presents and do each other kindnesses, and are far from sure who is the giver and who is the taker. This kind of shared concern is more than obliging co-operation. A close relationship between two ordinary human beings, as experienced, can amount to a unity in which their separate characters are not lost but enhanced.[10]

When we say, for instance, that a husband and wife are a united couple, we do not mean anything at all like mystical union. Their lives are joined, but not their identities. These people depend upon each other, though they are still separate people. The idea that to hurt or please one hurts or pleases the other is simple enough for children to understand. Their unity is not a matter of feeling obliged to be loyal, but of belonging to one another. To say that they are 'at one' is not a mere metaphor: if metaphors are mere.

So the unity-in-plurality of the Trinity is not unfounded in human life, when human life becomes what it ought to be: in other words, when human beings love each other. We have on the one hand a difficult theological doctrine, which was developed to account for what Jesus Christ had come to mean to Christians. We have on the other hand an aspect of human life which is somewhat mysterious when we stop to think about it, but which, unlike the Threefoldness of God, is entirely familiar. We arrived at these notions quite separately, so it is significant if they turn out to shed light upon one another.

It means more to be One God than to be one couple. The unity of Father, Son and Spirit must be closer than the unity of the dearest friends or the most devoted husband and wife; but the unity of human beings can help to show what the Three-in-

Oneness of God means by making it less paradoxical. Questions like 'Did God come? Or did the Father stay up in heaven and send His Son to suffer and die?' 'Is the Spirit really a separate person from Jesus?' lose a good deal of their sting when love, as we sometimes see it among human beings, is included in the equations.

This kind of illustration seems to make God more Three than One. Since early days, some Christians have found it more helpful to emphasize the unity of God, and think of one Being with three aspects: others have found it more helpful to think of three Beings united in love. Unfortunately Christian theologians themselves have been far from united in love, and have accused one another of heresy, both ways.

No Christian who wants to be loyal to our Jewish origins may sit light to the Oneness of God. To emphasize the Three-ness makes people nervous because it can sound like belief in three Gods, 'Tritheism'. There is no need to set theories against each other: rather it is a matter of deciding where to start. Although, or even because, our ancestors learnt first that God is One, there is a lot to be said now for attending particularly to the Three.[11]

To speak about God as Father, Son and Spirit began as a way of fitting Jesus in to Jewish monotheism. Once brought in, the doctrine can enrich our faith by showing us that love is built in to God's very existence. If 'God is Love', God must love somebody. So does God need creatures, to be the God Christians believe in? The doctrine that God is not just 'One and all alone' builds loving into God's very being. The God we worship has a life beyond our lives. This is no debating point. We are like children whose parents love each other, not lapdogs whose role is to give a lonely soul an interest in life.

The Trinity may be imagined as the life of God going on, irrespective of human arguments.[12] As the British Council of Churches Report called *The Forgotten Trinity* put it, 'God is a community consisting in unbroken personal relationships. This was a new and unique contribution to thought.'[13] If we want to talk about the 'social Trinity', so be it. To say that human beings are invited to join in God's heavenly life means more if we are sure that God's love is perfectly complete already and we are included out of sheer grace.

In thy light shall we see light[14]

Christians should not, and need not, let the Holy Trinity be 'forgotten'. The 'wise and understanding' are inclined to tie themselves in knots, but it seems to fit with the teaching of Christ to suppose that the mystery may be easier, not harder, for the less sophisticated.[15] Beginners, including any of us, can think about the Trinity as God the Father above us, God the Son with us, and God the Holy Spirit within us. Far from being an unnecessary complication, this simple scheme can give faith a firmer basis. There is no need to struggle to invent one's own God, or to lift oneself up to spiritual heights.

The God Christians believe in is there carrying them, whether they know it or nor and indeed whether they like it or not. The life of God is going on anyway: people have only to join in. If they say, as well they may, 'How do you know?' the answer is still 'Try it and see.' 'O taste, and see, how gracious the Lord is.'[16] This is not the sort of thing to prove, except by a lifetime of trying to live by it.

For many people, the Father and the Son seem fairly straightforward, but the Spirit is more puzzling, just because the Spirit evidently meant so much to the first Christians. If we take the New Testament emphasis on living 'in the Spirit' seriously, does that have to mean stirring ourselves up to be 'charismatics' in the specialized sense? It is not just laziness or cowardice which holds us back. People are not to be reckoned as second-class Christians if they find the idea of dancing in the aisles profoundly alien.

For quieter believers, the Holy Spirit can be less conspicuous and no less real. There is no need to doubt that God inspiring us within might make us feel like dancing for joy: but the main point to take hold of is that the Spirit shows us things. In the Society of Friends, the Spirit is the Inner Light. What we see *by*, is not so easy to look *at*. The headlamps of other cars only dazzle us. We are not called upon to stare at our source of illumination but to pay attention to whatever we can see. When we do attend we can expect to be shown things.

Christians are apt to expect prayer to be easy, because they have grasped the idea that Jesus taught his disciples to pray to God as Father. When disciples today try to obey, they may be quite discouraged to realize how big the gap is between first-century Galilee and themselves. God the Father can seem almost as far away as God the Almighty Creator. It is a great waste to stick at this point with half-shut eyes, and not see that the gap is bridged. If God is also Holy Spirit, we are more in touch than we think.

St Paul, whom we might imagine as settled comfortably on the heavenly side of the gap, said plainly 'we do not know how to pray as we ought': except that the Spirit joins in.[17] To call God 'Abba, Father' is not something we are supposed to manage for ourselves.[18] The practical meaning of belief in the Trinity is that God is on our side. What is asked of Christians is to consider themselves invited to take part in the life of heaven. We may imagine eternal life as a feast, or a conversation, or maybe as a dance, but the point is that it is going on anyway and each of us is allowed to contribute.[19]

If we can explain what we hope for in this sort of way, there is no need to fret about how little we can see now. We have hints and glimpses to go on with. Austin Farrer suggested an image of heaven as exploring God's mind, 'as we may explore the beautiful variety of a mountain country. We cannot explore all of it, but we can go where we like.'[20] In the meantime, we can encourage one another. 'Welcome one another, therefore, as Christ has welcomed you, for the glory of God.'[21]

Some Encouraging Books

A Book of English Belief: Bede to Temple, chosen by Joanna
 M. Hughes, SCM Press 1989
By Heart: A Lifetime Companion, selected and edited by John
 Bowden, SCM Press 1984
The Book of Common Prayer: The Psalms

John Austin Baker, *The Foolishness of God*, Darton, Longman
 and Todd 1970
James Barr, *The Bible in the Modern World*, SCM Press
 1973
D. J. Bartholomew, *God of Chance*, SCM Press 1984
Wesley Carr, *Brief Encounters*, SPCK 1985
Trevor Dennis, *Lo and Behold*, SPCK 1991
James D. G. Dunn, *The Evidence for Jesus*, SCM Press 1985
Austin Farrer, *A Science of God?* Bles 1966
*The Forgotten Trinity: the Report of the BCC Study Commis-
 sion on Trinitarian Doctrine Today*, British Council of
 Churches 1989
E. H. Gombrich, *Art and Illusion: a study in the psychology of
 pictorial representation*, Phaidon Press 1960
Morna Hooker, *St Mark*, A. & C. Black 1991
David Jenkins, *The Glory of Man*, SCM Press 1967
Julian of Norwich, *Showings*
Mary Midgley, *Beast and Man: the Roots of Human Nature*,
 Harvester 1978
Jürgen Moltmann, *Theology and Joy*, SCM Press 1973
*Mud and Stars: the impact of hospice experience on the
 church's ministry of healing*, Report of a working party,
 Sobell Publications 1991
John V. Taylor, *The Primal Vision*, SCM Press 1963; Xpress
 Reprints 1994
Thomas Traherne, *Centuries*

W. H. Vanstone, *Love's Endeavour, Love's Expense*, Darton, Longman and Todd 1977

Vernon White, *Atonement and Incarnation: an essay in universalism and particularity*, CUP 1991

Notes

Some of the questions in this book have been in my head for years. Sometimes I have summarized, sometimes expanded, and in a couple of cases quoted what I have said before; so it seemed best to make a numbered list of earlier books and articles and refer to these in the Notes by my initials, LHO.

(i) *Law and Love*, Faith Press 1962

(ii) *Incarnation and Immanence*, Hodder and Stoughton 1973

(iii) *The Hope of Happiness*, SCM Press 1983

(iv) *Looking Before and After*: The Archbishop of Canterbury's Lent Book for 1988, Collins Fount

(v) *Marriage* (in series 'Ethics: our choices'), Mowbray 1990

(vi) 'Mission, morals and folk religion', *Crossroads are for Meeting. Essays on the mission and common life of the church in a global society* SPCK/USA 1986

(vii) 'Making God findable', *The Parish Church?* ed. Giles Ecclestone, The Grubb Institute, Mowbray 1988

(viii) 'Grievances', *Theology*, January 1988

(ix) 'Spirit and Body', *Theology*, March/April 1990

(x) 'Blessing', *The Weight of Glory: Essays for Peter Baelz* ed. D. W. Hardy and P. H. Sedgwick, T. & T. Clark 1991

(xi) 'Belonging and the Individual', TRUST 5, December 1991

(xii) 'On the Maleness of Christ', *Theology*, November/December 1993

1. *Children Finding God?*

1. Sellars and Yeatman, *1066 and All That*, Methuen 1930, p. 63
2. Ps. 34.8
3. Cf. Basil Mitchell, 'Indoctrination', *How to Play Theological Ping-Pong*, Hodder and Stoughton 1990
4. Cf. LHO (iv), pp. 129, 133–5, 148
5. Mark 10.27

2. Behaving

1. David Jenkins, *What is Man?*, SCM Press 1970, p. 121
2. C. S. Lewis, *The Screwtape Letters*, Bles 1942, ch. 23
3. Ex. 20.1–17; Deut. 5.6–21
4. Eph. 3.18
5. Cf. LHO (iii), ch. 6
6. Ibid., ch. 7
7. Wordsworth, Sonnet: 'The inside of King's College Chapel, Cambridge'
8. Luke 10.30–37; 15.11–32
9. Matt. 13.3; Mark 4.3; Luke 8.5
10. Matt. 20.1–16

3. Believing

1. Austin Farrer, *A Science of God?*, Bles 1966, p. 10
2. Mark 9.24
3. John 20.25
4. John 20.8
5. Job 19.25
6. I Peter 3.15
7. Cf. Basil Mitchell, *The Justification of Religious Belief*, Macmillan 1973, ch. 3
8. Ps. 34.8
9. *Showings*, ch. 8
10. Matt. 6.6
11. Luke 12.32
12. John Lucas, 'Doubt', *Freedom and Grace*, SPCK 1976, pp. 121, 125
13. Robert Browning, 'Bishop Blougram's Apology'
14. Luke 2.46
15. Ps. 93.1
16. Eph. 6.13
17. John 3.1–12
18. Matt. 6.25–34
19. Mark 4.38
20. E.g. Matt 8.5–13; Mark 7.25–30
21. Matt. 18.3
22. Mark 4.40
23. Cf. C. S. Lewis, *The Screwtape Letters*, ch. 6
24. Lewis Carroll, *Through the Looking Glass*, ch. 2

4. *Cornerstone*

1. See above, p. 15
2. II Cor. 5.19
3. Matt. 12.42; Luke 11.31
4. Ps. 19.10
5. Matt. 11.19; Luke 7.34. Cf. Lord Hailsham, *The Door Wherein I Went*, Collins 1975, p. 54
6. E.g. Matt. 7.28–9; Mark 1.22, 27; 4.41; Luke 4.36; 8.25
7. Mark 10.32
8. Cf. Frances Young, *The Making of the Creeds*, SCM Press 1991
9. Dorothy L. Sayers, caricaturing the 'Athanasian' Creed: *Creed or Chaos*, Methuen 1947, p. 22
10. From Edwin Muir, 'One foot in Eden', *Collected Poems 1921–1958*, Faber and Faber 1960, p. 227. The biblical reference is Matt. 13.24–30
11. Gen. 3.5
12. John 14.6
13. John 21.21–2
14. See above, p. 18
15. Ludwig Wittgenstein, *Philosophical Investigations*, Blackwell 1953, para. 43: 'for a *large* class of cases – though not for all – in which we employ the word "meaning" it can be defined thus: the meaning of a word is its use in the language.'
16. Cf. LHO (vi), p. 50
17. See above, p. 16
18. Eph. 2.20
19. J. A. Baker, *The Foolishness of God*, Darton, Longman and Todd 1970, p. 311: cf. LHO (ii), pp. 59–9
20. Ibid., p. 54
21. Luke 16.31
22. II Cor. 5.19

5. *Finding God in Creation*

1. J. A. Baker, *The Foolishness of God*, p. 52
2. Laplace's reply to Napoleon's enquiry about the Creator
3. Stephen W. Hawkings, *A Brief History of Time*, Bantam Press 1988, p. 175
4. Deut. 6.4
5. Ps. 8.3
6. C. S. Lewis, *The Screwtape Letters*, ch. 1
7. I owe this way of putting it to my son-in-law, Ivo Mosley
8. Ps. 104.24

9. Ps. 104.25
10. Iris Murdoch, *The Sovereignty of Good*, Routledge 1970, p. 84; and cf. LHO (iii), p. 66
11. Augustine, *City of God* XII 4
12. Matt. 18.3
13. Ps. 65.5, 8
14. Thomas Traherne, *Centuries*, I 29
15. Cf. P. Baelz, *Does God Answer Prayer?*, Darton, Longman and Todd 1982, p. 31
16. Augustine, *Confessions* X vi
17. Ps. 104.26
18. The same verse in the Jerusalem Bible translation
19. Cf. John Stuart Mill, *Autobiography*, 1873, ch. 5
20. Cf. LHO (iv), pp. 119–25
21. Cf. LHO (iii), ch. 19
22. Mark 10.16
23. Ivo Mosley (ed), *The Green Book of Poetry*, Frontier Publishing 1993
24. Cf. Mary Midgley, *Beast and Man: the Roots of Human Nature*, Harvester 1978
25. Gen. 1.27
26. Gen. 1.2
27. Cf. LHO (iv), pp. 142–3
28. E. H. Gombrich, *Art and Illusion: a study in the psychology of pictorial representation*, Phaidon Press 1960
29. Ibid., pp. 34–6
30. Ibid., p. 186
31. Ibid., pp. 361f.
32. Ibid., pp. 335–6
33. Ibid., p. 202
34. See above, p. 39

6. *Finding God in Providence?*

1. W. B. Yeats, 'He Wishes for the Cloths of Heaven'
2. Ps. 40.1
3. W. M. Thackeray, *Vanity Fair*, 1847–8, ch. 66
4. Jer. 17.9
5. Lewis Carroll, *Alice's Adventures in Wonderland*, ch. 8
6. Luke 13.4
7. William Dunbar, 'Lament for the Makers'
8. Ps. 37.25
9. Matt. 28.46; Mark 15.34
10. Augustine, *On the Psalms*, Third discourse on Psalm 36 (37)

11. Mark 10.27
12. Matt. 7.7–11; Luke 11.5–13
13. Matt. 7.9
14. Matt. 6.30; Luke 12.28
15. Matt. 6.11; Luke 11.3
16. *epiousion*
17. John 14.13–4; 15.16; 16.23–7
18. Robert Browning, 'By the Fireside'
19. Rom. 8.22
20. Matt. 26.39; Mark 13.36; Luke 22.42
21. Ps. 118.23
22. Matt. 13.28
23. W. H. Vanstone, *Loves's Endeavour, Love's Expense*, Darton, Longman and Todd 1977, p. 65

7. *The Creator who Takes Risks*

1. Ps. 46.6
2. John Macquarrie, *Principles of Christian Theology*, SCM Press 1966, 1977
3. *Macbeth*, V 7
4. Ps. 100.2
5. Ps. 115.2
6. Austin Farrer, *A Science of God?* p. 76
7. Cf. John Macquarrie, *Principles of Christian Theology*
8. Austin Farrer, *A Science of God?*, p. 90
9. But cf. D. J. Bartholomew, *God of Chance*, SCM Press 1984
10. Rom. 8.22
11. See W. H. Vanstone, *Love's Endeavour, Love's Expense*
12. See below, e.g. p. 96
13. See above, pp. 20–21; cf. LHO (ii), pp. 1–2
14. Ps. 74.21
15. Mark 10.17–22
16. Cf. LHO (vi), p. 58
17. Letter to Melanchthon

8. *Finding Grace*

1. Austin Farrer, *Saving Belief*, Hodder and Stoughton 1967, p. 57
2. See below e.g., pp. 83ff
3. See above, p. 39
4. See above, p. 24

5. Isa. 53.6
6. See above, p. 45
7. See above, p. 24
8. See below, chs 16 & 17
9. I am grateful to Professor T. F. Torrance for reminding me of this argument
10. Ps. 42.9
11. Ps. 46.1
12. See above, pp. 20–21 and ch. 7 n. 13
13. *King Lear*, I 1
14. Isa. 45.15

9. *Enough to Go On*

1. See above, p. 16
2. George Herbert (1593–1633), 'Denial'
3. Cf. LHO (ii), pp. 52–3
4. Cf. ibid., p. 54
5. I Cor. 13.12
6. C. S. Lewis, *Surprised by Joy*, Bles 1955, pp. 63–4
7. Austin Farrer, *The Glass of Vision*, Bampton lectures for 1948, Dacre Press 1948, p. 7
8. Ibid., p. 8
9. Cf. LHO (ii), pp. 81–2
10. Matt. 5.8
11. Ex. 33.18–23
12. Gregory of Nyssa, *The Life of Moses*, paragraph 252
13. John 21.22
14. E.g. Gen. 2.12–3
15. Samuel Butler (1612–80), *Hudibras*
16. Cf. LHO (iii), pp. 16, 24
17. Bishop Butler, *Fifteen Sermons* (1729) III, paragraph 3
18. Eph. 5.20
19. See above, pp. 56, 69, 73
20. Antony Flew, 'Theology and Falsification' in Flew and MacIntyre (eds), *New Essays in Philosophical Theology*, SCM Press 1955, pp. 96–9
21. Ibid., p. 97
22. R. L. Stevenson, *Travels with a Donkey in the Cevennes*, 1879, (end of chapter called 'A night among the pines')
23. Ps. 115.1
24. *Henry V*, IV 8
25. Matt. 10.29
26. E.g. the Revised Standard Version and the New English Bible; but the

NOTES

latest revisions of these change back to 'apart from your Father' and 'without your Father's knowledge'; and the Jerusalem Bible has 'without your Father knowing'

27. John Keats, Letter to Benjamin Bailey, 22.11.1817
28. Sacks, *The Times*, 8.5.93
29. Rudolph Otto, *The Idea of the Holy*, 2nd edn, OUP 1950, Appendix VIII, p. 214. Cf. LHO (ii), p. 194
30. Cf. Jean-Pierre de Caussade (1675–1751), *Self-Abandonment to Divine Providence*
31. Ps. 139.7
32. Francis Thompson, 'The Hound of Heaven'
33. See above, pp. 17, 75
34. See above, p. 76; cf. LHO (iv), pp. 52–3
35. I Peter 3.15

10. *Finding God in Christ*

1. Edwin Muir, 'Prometheus', *Collected Poems 1921–1958*, Faber 1960, p. 216
2. See above, p. 35
3. There are many books on the history of Christian doctrine; e.g. Frances Young, *The Making of the Creeds*, SCM Press 1991
4. Phil. 2.8; cf. LHO (vii)
5. 'Christmas' from *John Betjeman's Collected Poems*, Enlarged Edition, John Murray 1970, p. 188
6. T. S. Eliot, 'Gerontion', *Collected Poems 1909–1962*, Faber 1963, p. 39
7. Austin Farrer, *Interpretation and Belief*, SPCK 1976, pp. 134–37
8. Matt. 4.3; Luke 4.3
9. Luke 4.13
10. E.g. James D. G. Dunn, *Unity and Diversity in the New Testament*, 2nd edn, SCM Press 1990
11. This view was propounded by St Anselm (1033–1109) in *Cur Deus homo*

11. *God With Us*

1. Cf. LHO (vi), pp. 49–50
2. See above, p. 47
3. Cf. LHO (iii), p. 50
4. Matt. 27.46; Mark 15.34
5. I Cor. 2.16

177

6. Luke 23.34, 43, 46; John 19.26–7, 28, 30
7. See above, p. 47
8. Mark 2.7; Luke 5.21
9. Cf. LHO (vi), p. 49
10. Cf. LHO (iii), p. 187
11. Cf. LHO (iv), ch. 8
12. Luke 9.50; cf. Mark 9.40
13. I Cor. 15.3–8
14. I Cor. 15.44
15. Ps. 16.10; Acts 2.27, 13.35
16. Cf. LHO (iv), pp. 99–101

12. *Finding God in Church*

1. This comes from one of the prayers after communion, in the Book of Common Prayer and in Rite B of the Alternative Service Book, from which the next few headings are also taken.
2. I Cor. 12.27; cf. e.g. Rom. 12.5; Eph. 5.23; Col. 1.18
3. Matt. 18.20
4. Ps. 34.8
5. Cf. Bruno Bettelheim, *A Good Enough Parent*, Thames and Hudson 1987
6. See above, p. 16
7. Matt. 6.27
8. Matt. 27.46; Mark 15.34; and Ps. 22.1
9. See above, p. 94
10. Cf. LHO (iii), p. 185
11. *Celebrating Common Prayer*, Mowbray 1992
12. Cf. LHO (xi), pp. 2–4
13. Isa. 53.6
14. Cf. LHO (ii), ch. 8
15. C. S. Lewis, *Mere Christianity*, Bles 1952, p. 147
16. Cf. LHO (iii), ch. 11
17. E.g. A. M. Allchin, 'The sacrament of marriage in Eastern Christianity', Appendix 3 of *Marriage, Divorce and the Church* (Root Report), SPCK 1971, p. 116; Vladimir Lossky, *In the Image and Likeness of God*, St Vladimir's Seminary Press 1974, Mowbrays 1974, p. 185; John D. Zizioulas, *Being as Communion: studies in personhood and the church*, St Vladimir's Seminary Press 1985, p. 113
18. E.g. I Cor. 12.27
19. E.g. Luke 14.26; Matt. 12.48–9; Mark 3.33–4
20. Cf. LHO (i)

13. Belonging

1. Cf. LHO (vii)
2. Voltaire: 'The best is the enemy of the good.' *Dictionnaire philosophique* (1764)
3. Luke 14.18
4. Rev. 3.16
5. This paragraph comes from a short article I wrote in the *Church Times*, 7.12.90
6. Gal. 6.2
7. See above, p. 16
8. See Frank Colquhoun, *Parish Prayers*, Hodder and Stoughton 1967, p. 249
9. II Peter 3.16; this paragraph also comes from the *Church Times* article, 7.12.90
10. Oliver Quick commended the 'principle of representative dedication'; *Essays in Orthodoxy*, Macmillan 1916, Chapter IX 9
11. Cf. LHO (vii), pp. 72–3, quoting from (vi), p. 54
12. Matt. 5.48
13. Matt. 6.5
14. Matt. 6.6
15. John 7.49
16. I learnt this way of putting it from Canon Lawrence Hibbs
17. Cf. LHO (xi), p. 4
18. The Catechism in the Book of Common Prayer
19. Cf. LHO (x), p. 227
20. Cf. Dalby, *Open Baptism*, SPCK 1989
21. Rom. 13.14; Gal. 3.27
22. Lewis Carroll, *Alice's Adventures in Wonderland*, ch. 10

14. Finding God in the Bible

1. James Barr, *The Bible in the Modern World*, SCM Press 1973, p. 123
2. Rom. 15.4
3. Matt. 23.9
4. See e.g. James Barr, *The Bible in the Modern World*; and John Barton, *What is the Bible?*, SPCK Triangle 1991. Cf. LHO (i), p. 91; (v), p. 40; (vii), p. 74
5. See above, p.89 and ch. 10 n. 10
6. Cf. S. Sykes, *Christian Theology Today*, Mowbray 1971, 1983, p. 73
7. E. g. Trevor Dennis, *Lo and Behold*, SPCK 1991
8. Rom. 15.4
9. I Cor. 2.16
10. Isa. 57.15

11. Matt. 12.40
12. I. T. Ramsey, *Religious Language*, SCM Press 1957 (Reissued Xpress Reprints 1993), e.g. p.23
13. LHO (iii), p. 181
14. E.g. I Sam. 20
15. II Sam. 1.17–27
16. II Sam. 11–12.25
17. II Sam. 13–19.8
18. Cf. LHO (iii), p. 181
19. Gen. 27.1–40; 32.3–24
20. Gen. 32.23–31
21. E.g. Gen. 17
22. Ex. 3–4.17
23. I Sam. 17
24. I Sam. 16.1–13; II Sam. 2.4
25. Amos 5.18
26. Ps. 137.4
27. E.g. Mark 5.25–34; 10.13–16; 12.41–4
28. E.g. Matt. 8.5–13; Mark 7.25–30; Luke 17.15–19
29. E.g. Luke 7.37–50; 19.1–10
30. E.g. Matt. 26.56; Mark 15.50
31. Heb. 13.6
32. Gen. 18.1
33. Gen. 19.1–9
34. Gen. 18.4–5
35. Ps. 65.4
36. E.g. Matt. 22.1–10
37. John 2.1–11
38. E.g. Rom. 12.13
39. Matt. 14.15–21; Mark 6.35–44; Luke 9.12–17; John 6.5–14; Matt. 15.29–39; Mark 8.1–10
40. Matt. 26.17–29; Mark 14.12–25; Luke 22.14–38; John 13–17; I Cor. 11.23–5
41. Luke 24.28–35
42. John 21.9–14
43. E.g. Mark 2.15–17; Luke 19.1–19
44. Matt. 8.11; Mark 14.25; Luke 13.29–30
45. George Herbert, 'Love'
46. See above, pp. 20, 33, 86
47. See above, p. 76
48. Heb. 1.3; cf. Col. 1.15
49. New Revised Standard Version
50. Revised English Bible

51. Cf. LHO (iii), ch. 17 esp. p. 154
52. Gen. 1.27
53. Matt. 28.16–20; Luke 24.50–1; cf. John 20.22; cf. LHO (iv), p. 100
54. Acts 1.9–11
55. Eph. 4.10

15. *Finding God in People*

1. E.g. Mark 1.14; John 4.23–4
2. John 10.7
3. John 14.6
4. E.g. Matt. 5.1–11; 7.21, 28–9; 12.49; Mark 1.14–15; 2.5–12; 10.42–5, 51–2; 12.28–34; Luke 6.46–9; 7.22; 8.25; 22.60–2; John 4.27; 9.24–5; 12.27–8
5. Matt. 25.31–40
6. Cf. LHO (iii), p. 130; (viii), e.g. p. 36
7. Acts 9.4–5; 26.14–5
8. Matt. 25.41–6
9. Matt. 25.34
10. Luke 10.30–7
11. Gerard Manley Hopkins (1844–1889), 'As kingfishers catch fire, dragonflies dráw fláme'
12. See above, pp. 107, 111, 114
13. Matt. 25.40
14. Matt. 25.35–6
15. Translation by Kuno Meyer, *Selections from Ancient Irish Poetry*, Constable 1913, p. 25
16. Cf. LHO (ii), p. 19
17. See above, p. 134
18. See above, p. 76
19. Heb. 4.12–13; c.f. LHO (ii), p. 106
20. Ps. 139.1
21. SCM Press 1963
22. Cf. LHO (ii), pp. 17f.; and ch. 18 below
23. Cf. LHO (ii), ch. 11
24. Col. 1.19
25. Luke 2.52
26. Matt. 28.20
27. Col. 1.17
28. E.g. Rom. 8.10; II Cor. 5.17; Gal. 2.20
29. E.g. John 15.4–11
30. *On the Psalms*: Fourth Discourse on Psalm 30, paragraph 8 (our Ps. 31.22)

16. *Finding God in Things*

1. Cf. LHO (ii), ch. 2; (iv), chs 4 and 5; (ix), pp. 135–6
2. See above, pp. 126, 130–32
3. Ps. 34.8
4. Cf. LHO (ii), pp. 99–102; (iii), pp. 90–1; (iv), pp. 63–4) (vii), pp. 75–6; (ix), p. 137–9; (x), p. 226
5. See his sonnet, 'God's Grandeur'
6. 'Aurora Leigh', Book 7. The reference is to Ex. 3.5
7. Book of Common Prayer, the Catechism
8. Cf. LHO (vi), p. 63; (vii), p. 76
9. I owe this clarification to P. J. Fitzpatrick, *In Breaking of Bread*, CUP 1993
10. E.g. John 6.50–9
11. P. J. Fitzpatrick, *In Breaking of Bread*, e.g. p. 124
12. Ibid., e.g. p. 256
13. Cf. LHO (ii), pp. 99–102
14. See below, pp. 154–5
15. See above, pp. 130–32
16. *Macbeth*, I 7
17. Michael Sadgrove, 'Companions of Christ: a sermon on Maundy Thursday', *Theology*, March/April 1993, p. 128.
18. Gillian Feeley-Harnik, 'Meals', *The Oxford Companion to the Bible*, OUP 1993, p. 507
19. Gen. 18.8 (and above p. 130)
20. Ps. 50.12–13
21. See Lawrence A. Hoffmann, 'Rabbinic *Berakah* and Jewish spirituality', *Asking and Thanking* ed. Christian Duquoc and Casiano Florestan, *Concilium* 1990/3; cf. LHO (x), p. 224
22. See above, p. 84
23. Ps. 50.10

17. *The Breaking of Bread*

1. E.g. Matt. 4.2; John 4.7
2. Matt. 11.19; Luke 7.34
3. Mark 5.43; Luke 8.55
4. Matt. 8.15; Mark 1.31; Luke 4.39
5. Mark 3.20
6. See above, p. 131
7. Matt. 14.15–21; Mark 6.35–44; Luke 9.12–17; John 6.5–14; Matt. 15.29–39; Mark 8.1–10

8. Mark 6.41
9. See ch. 16 n. 21
10. I Cor. 11.23–5
11. Ps. 104.15
12. *anamnesis*
13. Austin Farrer, 'The Eucharist in I Corinthians', *Eucharistic Theology Then and Now*, SPCK Theological Collections No. 9, 1968, p. 31
14. Cf. LHO (ii), p. 102
15. See above, pp. 97–9
16. Luke 24.30–1
17. Luke 24.41–3
18. John 21.12
19. See above, p. 134
20. John Betjeman, 'Christmas'
21. Gillian Feeley-Harnik, 'Meals', *The Oxford Companion to the Bible*, OUP 1993, p. 507. She points out, 'Food, articulated in meals, was the embodiment of God's word, divine Wisdom, for people who would have no graven images.'
22. Acts 2.42
23. Cf. LHO (ii), p. 102
24. Gregory Dix, *The Shape of the Liturgy*, Dacre Press 1945, p. 744
25. *Richard II*, I 1, lines 139–41
26. Daniel Brevint, *The Christian Sacrament and Sacrifice*, I 1
27. Ibid., I 2
28. Ibid., II 9
29. Cf. LHO (ix), p. 139. See above, p. 87
30. 'The mass on the world', *Hymn of the Universe*, Collins 1965, p. 19; cf. LHO (ix), p. 137
31. See above, p. 118; cf. Ross Thompson, 'Christian initiation as a Trinitarian process', *Theology*, March/April 1994. Cf. Anne Primavesi and Jennifer Henderson, *Our God has no Favourites*, Burns and Oates 1989

18.   God the Holy Trinity

1. Robert Browning, 'An Epistle Containing the Strange Medical experience of Karshish the Arab Physician'
2. See above, p. 28
3. Gen. 1.2; Mark 1.10
4. *The Forgotten Trinity: the Report of the BCC Study Commission on Trinitarian Doctrine Today*, British Council of Churches 1989, Paragraph 5.1.2
5. See above, pp. 89, 124, 126; and James D. G. Dunn, *Unity and Diversity in the New Testament*

183

6. Isa. 46.4
7. C. S. Lewis, *The Screwtape Letters*, ch. 4
8. See above, p. 96
9. Cf. LHO (ii), ch. 11
10. Ibid., and p. 205
11. Ibid., pp. 204–7. See Leonard Hodgson, *The Doctrine of the Trinity*, Nisbet 1943, pp. 90ff.
12. See above, p. 161
13. *The Forgotten Trinity*, Paragraph 3.3
14. Ps. 36.9
15. Matt. 11.25; Luke 10.21
16. Ps. 34.8
17. Rom. 8.26
18. Rom. 8.15; Gal. 4.6; cf. LHO (ii), p. 111
19. See above, p. 161
20. Austin Farrer, 'Into the hands', *A Celebration of Faith*, Hodder and Stoughton 1970, p. 115
21. Rom. 15.7

Index

Ps. 40: 49; Ps. 42: 72;
Ps. 46: 57, 72; Ps. 50: 151;
Ps. 65: 39, 130–131; Ps. 74:
63; Ps. 93: 21; Ps. 100: 58;
Ps. 104: 37, 41, 47; Ps. 115:
59, 82; Ps. 118: 56; Ps. 139:
85, 141
putting on Christ, 12

QED, 16, 33
Quick, Oliver, 179

radicals, 18, 27, 29, 30–31,
124, 125
Ramsey, I. T., 128, 180
Raphael, 46, 149
reason for the hope, 16, 85
Redeemer, 'I know that my
Redeemer liveth', 15
redemption, 24, 56, 68
representing, 101, 107, 111,
114, 138–139, 145, 152
resurrection, rising, Christ
raised, 5, 8, 13, 31, 32, 34,
53, 63, 64, 65, 85, 86, 96–
99, 100, 102–103, 127, 130,
132, 155, 156; ours, 98–99
Risen Christ, 98, 133–135,
142, 156–157
reticence, 118
reverence, 6, 14, 27, 37–38,
55, 56, 58, 62, 88, 93, 94,
160
rich young man, 63
right and wrong, 10, 11, 78, 79
difference between, 9, 11
rigorism, 12, 120
rising, see resurrection

risk, 59, 60, 62–63
ritual, 71, 116, 146, 147, 154,
159
Robinson, J. A. T., 141
rules, 8, 12

Sabbath, 130
Sacks, Jonathan, 84
sacrament, 70–71, 100, 118,
146–148, 155, 159, 160,
161; and see eucharist, presence
sacrament of the present
moment, 84
sacrifice, 90, 95, 149, 151
Sadgrove, Michael, 182
Samaritan, 138
Sayers, Dorothy L., 29 and
note
sceptics, unbelievers, 7, 10, 11,
16, 18, 19, 21–22, 23, 32–
33, 53, 59, 62, 68, 76, 80,
81, 92
science, scientists, 3, 20, 28,
32–33, 35, 36–38, 60, 162
secret, Father who sees in, 118
secularism, 20, 31, 64, 65
self-righteousness, 12
Sermon on the Mount, 22, 53;
and see particular references
Shakespeare, 123; and see Cordelia, Henry V, Macbeth,
Mowbray
sheep, 'all we like', 70, 104
Shepherd, Good, 4, 21
showing, 11, 16, 39, 43, 45–
46, 68, 70, 77, 140, 164,
167–168